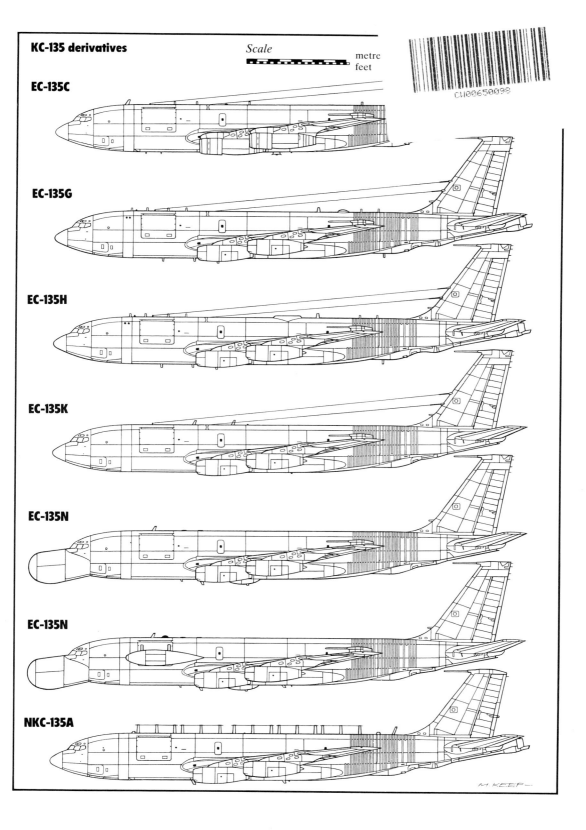

KC-135 derivatives

Scale

metre
feet

EC-135C

EC-135G

EC-135H

EC-135K

EC-135N

EC-135N

NKC-135A

M. KEEP

BOEING KC-135 STRATOTANKER

BOEING KC-135 STRATOTANKER

ROBERT F. DORR

00322

LONDON

IAN ALLAN LTD

Contents

First published 1987

ISBN 0 7110 1745 X

Published by Ian Allan Ltd, Shepperton, Surrey; and printed by Ian Allan Printing Ltd at their works at Coombelands in Runnymede, England

Previous page:
A classic view of the tanker. Boeing KC-135A Stratotanker 60-0322 lands at RAF Marham, England, in 1982. *John Dunnell*

Preface

In its primary role as an air refuelling tanker the Boeing KC-135 Stratotanker is unique. No other aircraft has performed the same function from so early, or for so long, or with so much success. But the KC-135 is more than a tanker. There exist no fewer than 60-odd variants of the KC-135, used for diverse roles and missions. In the limited space afforded by a volume of this nature, it becomes especially difficult to cover the full story of such a multi-faceted aircraft. A hint at the scale of the problem is provided by the chapter headings used here, which spell out a few of the principal roles of the KC-135.

For a story as diverse as this one, it becomes especially important to say that any mistakes are the fault of the author. This volume would have been impossible, however, without the generous help of many who assisted.

I owe a special debt to Clyde Gerdes who was one of the early KC-135 followers and who helped so many other authors, historians and photographers before his untimely death in 1981. This work is dedicated to Clyde.

I am especially grateful to publisher Simon Forty, to Marilyn Phipps of Boeing's historical division in Seattle, and to Col Claude Rossello, the C-135F pilot who serves as France's air attaché in London. Thanks are due to Reed Duncan, who

prepared the section on reconnaissance. I also would like to thank Robert J. Archer, Paul Bennett, Roger F. Besecker, Paul F. Crickmore, John Dunnell, Michael France, Emlyn Jones, David W. Menard, Douglas E. Slowiak, Jim Sullivan, Norman Taylor and Nicholas Williams.

The opinions expressed in this work are my own and do not necessarily reflect those of the Department of State or of the United States Air Force.

Robert F. Dorr

Below:
Familiar EC-135H 61-0285 was a routine sight to European aircraft spotters before and after acquiring the TF33 turbofan engines seen here. Operated by the 10th ACCS at RAF Mildenhall, the Stratotanker is depicted at RAF Fairford in 1985. This theatre command post flies the US flag on its rudder and retains its flying boom refuelling system. *John Dunnell*

Glossary

ACCS	Airborne Command & Control Squadron	SDI	Strategic Defense Initiative
AEAO	Airborne Emergency Actions Officer	SLAR	Sideways-Looking Airborne Radar
AFB	Air Force Base	SMILS	Sonobuoy Missile Impact Location System
ALCC	Airborne Launch Control Center	SRW	Strategic Reconnaissance Wing
ANG	Air National Guard	TAC	Tactical Air Command
ANGB	Air National Guard Base	UHF	ultra-high frequency
AREFS	Air Refueling Squadron	VHF	very high frequency
AREFW	Air Refueling Wing	VLF	very low frequency
ARIA	Apollo Range Instrumented Aircraft; later, Advanced Range Instrumented Aircraft	WRS	Weather Reconnaissance Squadron
ARS	Air Refueling Squadron		
ARW	Air Refueling Wing		
ASD	Aeronautical Systems Division		
A-LOTS	Airborne Lightweight Optical Tracking System		
AWACS/W	Airborne Warning And Control Squadron/Wing		
BMW	Bomb Wing		
EMP	electromagnetic pulse		
ETR	Eastern Test Range		
HEL	high-energy laser		
HF	high frequency		
ICBM	Intercontinental Ballistic Missile		
MAC	Military Airlift Command		
MATS	Military Air Transport Service		
MAW	Military Airlift Wing		
PACCS	Post-Attack Command & Control System		
SAC	Strategic Air Command		

Below:

From this angle, command post EC-135H 61-0285 shows its dorsal saddle aerial and blade, wire and wingtip probes. *John Dunnell*

1 The Mission

In my London flat, the phone rings. 'It's tomorrow', the voice says. It has taken months but I've gotten permission to go aloft in a Boeing KC-135 Stratotanker to refuel fighters high over Germany.

The air refuelling mission, the 'force multiplier' which enables bombers and fighters to stretch their legs and to reach targets far from home, is for me about to become a first-hand experience. It is a routine part of flight operations today, taken for granted in peacetime and included in all contingency plans for fighting a war. In fact it seems difficult to remember that air refuelling was not always taken for granted. There has been some form of refuelling on everyday operations since the 1950s but the air refuelling function didn't become a part of actual combat flying until the long and bitter struggle against Hanoi. In the South-East Asia conflict the tanker proved itself in the crucible.

On 3 May 1967 the shooting was still going on when two F-105 Thunderchiefs heading home from a pitched battle over North Vietnam found themselves too short on fuel to reach any base in the region. A tension settled over the Thud pilots. Storm clouds loomed around them. The airwaves were filled with panicked calls from other fighter pilots, many also low on fuel, others limping home with battle damage. Desperate, the two-plane Thud leader radioed for any tanker assistance he could get. In one of the classic foul-ups of the war, so many people tried to respond that the F-105 leader's earphones shrieked with voices, blocking out each other's transmissions. All the while, the leader and his wingman watched their fuel gauges keep sinking. In the best of times a tanker could routinely insert its 'flying boom' into the nose receptacle on the spine of an F-105 and pump life-giving fluid, but this was the height of the 'Rolling Thunder' campaign, the F-105 pilots had just mixed it up with missiles, MiGs and Triple-A, and their efforts to locate a tanker were being stymied by over-use of the radio channels. The two fighter pilots were in serious trouble.

Stratotanker in Combat

Maj Alvin K. Lewis and his crew, flying anchor orbit in a KC-135 in a distant area, monitored the confusing radio traffic. Though he was obstructed in his efforts to talk to the Thud pilots, Lewis managed to eke out enough information to turn towards their location. The silvery KC-135 appeared in front of the fighters, dangling high against the sun with a backdrop of green-brown Thai jungle, just as the F-105 leader was preparing

Below:
Heading out on a mission, the Strategic Air Command's standard air-refuelling tanker is an impressive sight. This KC-135 Stratotanker, taxi lights aglow, is moving on to the runway at RAF Greenham Common in July 1983.
John Dunnell

to eject. Lewis began an emergency-power diving bank from behind the F-105, got a break on the radio, and called the fighter jock to check his seven o'clock position.

Maj Lewis had to manoeuvre the huge 316,000lb (143,388kg) tanker frantically to achieve the hook-up. He 'latched on' to the Thud in a 20° dive while turning to the right just as the F-105 was flaming out for lack of fuel. In a precarious attitude, the tanker refuelled the fighter until it could restart, increasing the angle of the dive to 30° in the process. By then the second F-105 was in trouble so Lewis proceeded toward it. In moments he saved two Thunderchief crews who, but for his incredible skill at the controls, would certainly have had to eject.

Lewis's was but one of the inspiring sagas to come from the Vietnam conflict, the first war in which air refuelling was used routinely on combat missions. The first actual combat use of air refuelling had taken place during the 1950-53 Korean conflict — a primitive and shaky link-up between a prop-driven Boeing KB-29P Superfortress and a Republic F-84G Thunderjet — but this has been essentially a trial, albeit under fire. Since the Vietnam era the tanker mission, the primary role of the Boeing C-135 family yet only one of the many jobs performed by this aircraft, has become so routine as to receive far less attention than it deserves. Today's American forces, and those of the West, rely on air refuelling for virtually every aerial mission of any consequence.

Orientation Flight

Now it was my turn: 24 May 1984 was the date of my long-requested combat support mission mounted from RAF Mildenhall, England, by a Boeing KC-135A Stratotanker (59-1461), callsign

'Dobby 32', of the 380th Air Refueling Squadron, home-based at Plattsburgh AFB, New York. This required a 3am wake-up and a two-hour drive through fog-laced English countryside with a half-moon hanging over the trees, but at daybreak I was standing with aircraft commander Capt Karen M. Cunningham, watching the dawn splash over the great silvery Boeing. It scarely bears comment in today's world that the pilot of this Strategic Air Command giant was a woman.

Instead, my thoughts were focused on what an engineering marvel the KC-135 is, what an impressive sight it makes to the onlooker, and how erroneous it would be to take it for granted.

To get some 'feel' for the KC-135A — and this was the earliest, most basic model of an aircraft which has been built or converted into more variants than any other — the basic facts are hopelessly inadequate. Yes, the aircraft is 134ft 6in (40.99m) long, with a wingspan of 130ft 10in (39.88m), making it a big machine by any standard. Yes, power is provided by four 13,750lb (6.273kg) thrust Pratt & Whitney J57-P59W turbojets (on this variant), enabling the Strato-tanker to reach a maximum speed of 580mph (933km/hr), and to achieve a combat radius of 3,450 miles (5,552km). But after saying 'gee whiz', I felt the need for some other standard of measure, some other numbers, to describe this big silvery bird.

Fortunately, one such set of numbers was put together by an astute SAC public-affairs type, who discovered that the Boeing KC-135A Stratotanker does all of the following. It is worth setting down some of his unusual facts about the KC-135A. It:

● transfers enough fuel through its refuelling boom in one minute to operate the average passenger car for more than one year;
● uses 150gal of water for each water-injected take-off;
● contains enough material in the tyres of its landing gear (eight main wheels and two nose wheels) to produce 100 automobile tyres;
● requires 700 electronic tubes in its electronic system, enough to build 50 television sets, generating enough heat to supply a five-room house;
● carries 64 US gal of oil, enough for 50 automobiles, to lubricate its four jet engines;
● carries on a single flight enough fuel to last the average driver 46 years.

My tanker mission begins not on the hardstand where the KC-135A waits but in the ready room, while the sun is still working its way above the horizon and the crew is coping with vending machine coffee. The KC-135A carries a crew of four, and SAC uses hard crews, the same people flying together all the time. In addition to Capt Cunningham who occupies the left-hand pilot's seat and is unquestionably the boss, I am flying with co-pilot First Lieutenant Douglas E. Maple, navigator Capt Randall P. Callam, and boom operator Staff Sergeant Joseph P. Baka.

The 'Boomer'
The F-4 Phantom is 'the hardest aircraft to refuel', says Baka, who has refuelled almost every type

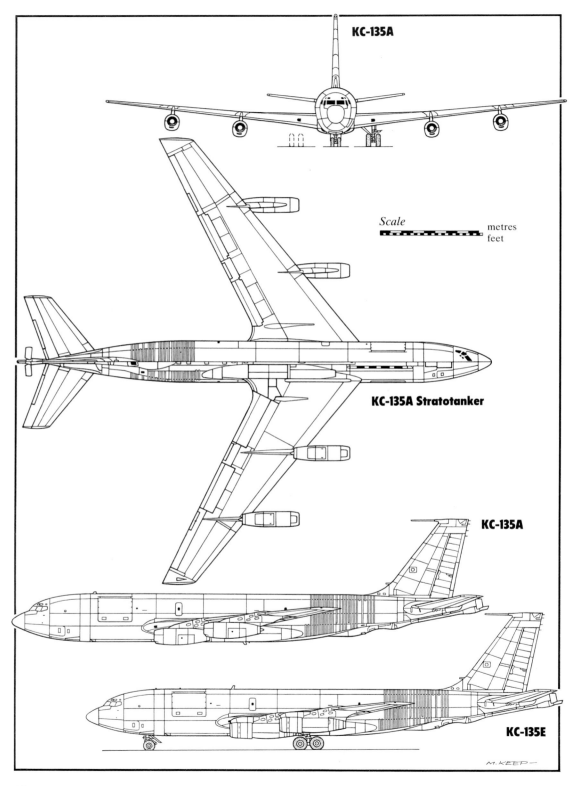

KC-135A

Scale metres feet

KC-135A Stratotanker

KC-135A

KC-135E

M. KEEP

and is not merely a 'boomer' but a qualified boom instructor. His job is to lie prone in the rear of the Stratotanker, peering backward and down through disappointingly small windows, and to operate the boom which will carry fuel to the tanker's receiving aircraft. The boomer is a special breed, a rigorously-trained, fiercely-proud non-commissioned officer who in some situations can become more important than the aircraft commander. With the success of the film *Star Wars* it is inevitable that Baka would be nicknamed 'Chew'.

We proceed to Base Operations to have a weather briefing and file a flight plan. Technical Sergeant Mary Hebert, who provides the former, has just received a 'weather person of the year' award. She talks of low pressure systems all over Europe. There are isolated thunderstorms up to 28,000ft (8,524m), and there's an 80% probability of encountering lightning. We will have an 8,000ft (2,438m) ceiling on take-off which will degrade to a 4,000ft (1,219m) ceiling by the time we are homeward bound from the planned three-hour

Top:
New Hampshire ANG KC-135E Stratotanker 59-1450 is here being readied for a mission in 1985. The open crew access door adjacent to the nosewheel is the only means of entering the aircraft. *New Hampshire ANG*

Above:
Take-off. KC-135A tanker 60-0313 launches with smoke trailing from its exhausts. Red and white vertical stripes on the tail in this 1984 view mark the aircraft as belonging to the 307th Air Refueling Squadron, part of SAC's 410th Bomb Wing, at K. I. Sawyer AFB, Michigan. *USAF*

mission. As always, where women and men rehearse for war in a European theatre where NATO and the Warsaw Pact confront each other, the weather is lousy.

On the bus ride to the flight line we chat. Baka says the 'weirdest receptacle' on a receiving aircraft belongs to the Lockheed C-141 Starlifter, since it curves upward, but he would rather refuel anything than an F-4. At one point he says to the

Above:
KC-135A Stratotanker 62-3552 of the 96th Bomb Wing, SAC, is seen at RAF Mildenhall, England, in 1983. The nose wheel has just been retracted but the wheel well door remains open. *Paul Bennett*

Right:
As seen from the receiver aircraft, the refuelling boom of the KC-135 Stratotanker is an impressive sight. This tanker, piloted by Lt-Col David Budge, is about to plug into a B-52 Stratofortress. *USAF*

Below:
During early service trials, a KC-135A Stratotanker (55-3135) employs the flying boom to refuel a Vought A-7D Corsair II (69-6189). Much of the credit for a successful refuelling must go to the enlisted boom operator, who lies prone, facing to the rear, and guides the meter process. *USAF*

ground crew, 'It's F-4s today, so grease up the boom'. It takes me a moment to understand that it is a joke, that they do not really use Vaseline to make the job easier. Baka says there is a point called 'decision contact' with fighters, the refuelling of fighters being different from other aircraft. How does it feel to fly in the 1,461st airframe, ordered by the US Air Force in fiscal year 1959, the year one of the crew members was born? 'They've been re-skinned.' Some KC-135As have a doppler navigation system which occupies considerable space on the flight deck, crowding in on the co-pilot. Alighting from the bus to pace towards 'Dobby 32' on the hardstand, we watch an SR-71 Blackbird run up its engines and take off.

Now the sun is up, Cunningham is serious, and there is no question who is in charge. She performs a quick walk-around check, not a thorough one so as not to insult the highly skilled maintenance crew who have kept 'Dobby 32' in flying mettle. (The notion of the pilot making a pre-flight is a basic in aviation; during the height of KC-135 combat support missions in Vietnam, it was ignored altogether.) 'In case we have to abandon the aircraft we'll meet at that little building over there' — she points — 'and do a count for five people on the airplane'.

We climb straight up into the KC-135A via the ladder going up from beside the nosewheel to the flight deck. Inside, there is a further briefing from Cunningham. Alarm bells are explained, egress techniques are explained. The parachutes are left hanging; no one will wear them today.

We're briefed on how to use oxygen in event of an explosive decompression. For the remainder of the mission I'll carry oxygen slung over one shoulder, getting it mixed up with my plug-in earphone set, camera bag and notebook — hard to keep it all straight. I do not receive a briefing on Callum's loose leaf notebook which is marked SECRET/NOFORN, nor on the padded thermal radiation shields which will seal off outside light if we find ourselves in a nuclear battle environment.

Everybody sits in the front cabin for take-off, me in the jump seat between Cunningham and the co-pilot. Cunningham is content to let Maple handle the radio traffic. We taxi out on the hardstand ahead of 'Dobby 33' and 'Ramon 23'. Cleared to cross the runway and turn at runway's end for run-up, the cabin crew do what all fliers do: crank their necks around looking for somebody in the approach pattern who isn't supposed to be there. 'Dobby 32' is cleared for take-off. Cunningham releases brakes and moves the throttles forward. We make an eventless take-off and climb out at a precariously steep angle.

Into the Mission
The skies are crowded over the Continent, a reminder of how intense the fighting will be if it ever comes. 'German Air Force 38 51' is on the radio waves heading for a nearby base and *that*, of course, is an F-4F Phantom. 'Rockville 14' is out there somewhere — perhaps another KC-135? I drop back to the boom operator's position, recline next to Baka, and look out just in time to see an F-104 shoot across our path from right to left, no more than 500ft (152m) below us. Moments later an F-15 goes past, upside-down! The airwaves are cluttered. Looking down at a floor of cloud thousands of feet below, Baka and I wonder where in hell are the receiver aircraft. An RF-4C appears and flies formation on us for a time, but he isn't ours. He seems to have packed the wrong tanker. He peels off, perhaps looking for 'Dobby 34'.

We're supposed to refuel 'Zerox' flight of RF-4C Phantoms from the 26th Tactical Reconnaissance Wing at Zweibrucken AB, Germany. But they aren't there! Just empty blue and a layer of white miles below.

The procedure for a mid-air rendezvous is well established. The tanker arrives at a dot on the map called the Air Refueling Control Point (ARCP). The intent is for the KC-135 to be at this point 15 minutes ahead of the receivers and to immediately begin a left-hand turn to fly a pattern that resembles a racetrack, called an anchor. Tanker and receivers approach each other head-to-head, the best way to avoid an inadvertent collision; when it makes contact and turns to lead the receivers, the KC-135A will confront them at a 26° left slant, at a distance of 21 miles (33.6km). Rendezvous is achieved with different equipment according to the receiver aircraft type; with the B-52 a radar beacon is employed, with most fighters it is UHF radio, with the RF-4C air-to-air TACAN. Ideally the tanker will commence the final elongated lap of the racetrack just as its receiver enters the same pattern, below the tanker and in position to refuel. Tanker and receivers will seek to complete the actual transfer of fuel while flying the straight, elongated portion of the anchor. In South-East Asia, predetermined anchors over Thailand and the South China Sea were given names like 'Mango', 'Lemon', 'Peach' and 'Cherry'. The larger regions in which the anchors were located had evocative names like 'Glass Top', 'Busy Rooster' and 'Saddle Soap'. On today's mission in the NATO arena, the anchor employed by Capt Cunningham in 'Dobby 32' is nicknamed, simply, 'William'. And the receiver aircraft, RF-4Cs, do not appear in 15 minutes. Nor do they appear in a half-hour. Nor in 45 minutes. 'Somebody's got their schedule mixed up', ponders Chew Baka. For reasons unknown, our RF-4C

Right:
Green and white diagonal stripes on the tail mark this KC-135A Stratotanker (60-0336) as belonging to the 310th Air Refueling Squadron, part of the 380th Bomb Wing at Plattsburgh AFB, New York. This standard tanker is seen in motion in early 1985. *USAF*

Above:
During the South-East Asia conflict, the sight of a KC-135A refuelling a B-52 Stratofortress became commonplace. This more recent view shows a weathered B-52 taking on fuel. *USAF*

Below:
KC-135A Stratotanker 61-4828 of the 509th Bomb Wing on let-down at RAF Mildenhall, England, in February 1985. The stripes on the rudder are blue and maroon.

Mildenhall is a familiar stop-over to KC-135A crews, who have been taking temporary deployments to the East Anglian airbase for many years. *Paul Bennett*

Bottom:
Fairchild AFB, Washington — spelled out on the tail of this KC-135A — is home base for 57-1419 and the 92nd Bomb Wing. It was seen during a visit to RAF Mildenhall, England, in May 1986. *Paul Bennett*

Phantom receivers, 'Zerox' flight, are still on the ground at Zweibrucken. Our three-hour mission will last five hours. 'Could a delay like this happen in wartime?' I ask.

Baka doesn't answer. Another day, another time, RF-4C Phantom squadron commander Lt-Col Carl Loveland will tell me that the real doubts are about the tankers, not the receivers. If the balloon goes up, NATO's fighter, strike and reconnaissance pilots will go to war not knowing if air refuelling, now taken so much for granted, will be there for them. *All* American tanker assets belong to SAC and therefore all available tankers could be diverted to feed SAC's bombers. And what about the fighter, strike and recce birds that don't belong to SAC, that depend on the KC-135A for sustenance, especially when assaulting Eastern Europe from bases as distant as the British Isles? Will the tankers be there for them? Does anyone even know? Loveland: 'I think it's legitimate to express doubt'.

For what seems an interminable period now, Karen Cunningham has held us in our anchor orbit, but still no Phantoms! Ground chatter reveals even now that they aren't aloft. It's cold. Prone, next to the boomer, my feet are freezing. Damned oxygen kit, earphones, camera, all kicking about and me wanting to take pictures at high speed through a 2ft window while wriggling next to Baka. Impossible! All this and no indication *when* . . .

'These things sometimes get delayed, y'know'.
'What if this were a war?'
'That's the point. It ain't'.

The Phantoms are an hour late. The mission is extended. But when they finally appear, what a sight!

'Zerox 76' (69-0368) is the first RF-4C to pull up under the boom, filling the sky beneath us. From atop Baka now, in a position that is awkward to describe and awkward to maintain, I am looking down from a distance of about 10ft, or 3m, at the visored, helmeted head of the RF-4C Phantom aircraft commander as he peers up at us and our fuel nozzle slips into the dorsal receptacle of his aircraft.

'Zerox' flight, originally to have been eight Phantoms, ends up being six — 69-0368, 69-0356, one unknown serial, 39-0366, 71-0251 and 72-0153. All are painted in wrap-around TO114 camouflage

Below:
Despite its enormous size, the Stratotanker handles very well during ground taxying. This KC-135A is making a turn at RAF Fairford, England, during the 1985 International Air Tattoo, a show which brought together more than a dozen of the Boeing tankers from around the world.
John Dunnell

Left:
Most KC-135 aircraft came off Boeing's production line with water-injection Pratt & Whitney J57 engines, which left sooty black smoke in their exhausts. The engines also seemed, in retrospect, rather small for the size of the aircraft. This KC-135A is taking off from the Renton plant. *Boeing*

Left:
The first major re-engining programme for the Stratotanker entailed retrofitting KC-135A aircraft with TF33 turbofans and redesignating them KC-135E. This KC-135E (57-1429) belongs to the 117th Air Refueling Squadron of the Kansas ANG and is visiting RAF Mildenhall, England, in March 1983. *Paul Bennett*

Left:
The most recent re-engining programme has entailed fitting Stratotankers with the huge CFM56 engines, seen here with access doors partially open, the aircraft being redesignated KC-135R. This R model (63-7999) belongs to the 384th Bomb Wing and is visiting RAF Mildenhall in 1986. *Paul Bennett*

with black serials and tailcodes. Some carry the new Phantom reconnaissance system known as TEREC. Like missile silo crews who prepare to launch ICBMs without knowing their targets, we refuel these aircraft not knowing what they will do after leaving us. If this were the real thing, they might be heading for post-strike recce on rail yards in Czechoslovakia or perhaps a look at a Frontal Aviation fighter strip in Germany. Who knows?

Surprisingly little radio chatter passes between Baka and the fighter pilots. Little is needed to mate two jet aircraft at high speed and altitude. While I look over Baka's shoulder, the KC-135A's full transfer load of 31,200gal of JP-4 fuel is delivered to the receiving aircraft at a rate of 1,000gal/min. Baka thanks the RF-4C pilot who lingers off-centre from the boom to give me a clear, sharp view of his aircraft. 'Sir, this pax is writing a book on the KC-135'.

As seen from the pilot of the receiver aircraft, the KC-135 looms overhead, filling the sky. The in-flight 'flex' of the tanker's 130ft 10in (40.99m) wing is readily evident from the front seat of the

Phantom. The RF-4C Phantom pilot literally flies into the boom, then hangs there. It happens around the clock, 24 hours a day, in good weather and bad, and mishaps are remarkably few.

SAC is, of course, rightly concerned about the danger of inadvertent collision during refuelling. In one such collision, the famous 'Palomares incident' over Spain on 17 January 1966 which caused the destruction of KC-135A 61-0273, the receiver B-52 Stratofortress dropped four hydrogen bombs, one of which subsequently had to be recovered from the depths of the Mediterranean. Needless to say, safety devices prevented the bombs from detonating, but collisions can and have killed people. In the early days of KC-135 operations, SAC's tankers were painted with bright orange Day-glo stripes around the front and back of the fuselage to assist the pilot of the receiver aircraft in adjusting visually to his own attitude relative to the tanker. It was determined from early experience that the orange trim was unnecessary.

Also gone now is the bright yellow stripe which was painted on the bottom of the KC-135 fuselage to assist the receiver pilot in aligning himself. This too was found superfluous. Still retained, however, are director lights which are arrayed in two parallel lines on the bottom of the KC-135 forward fuselage. Intended to aid the receiver pilot at night and in conditions of poor visibility, these are called, because of their shape, 'captain's bars'.

Homeward Bound

In a sense, the actual refuelling is an anti-climax. It takes only about 45 seconds to fill an RF-4C Phantom with fuel. The KC-135 does not permit visibility for more than one person through the small windows in the boomer's position (one of the few faults in the aircraft, and one corrected in abundance with the spacious boomer's compartments in the KC-10 Extender), so Sgt Baka and I are closer than we ever wanted to be. In order for me to see through the windows from his position (which forms a bulge or pod on the ventral side of the aircraft), I have to lie directly on top of the prone Baka and peer down over his shoulder. From this vantage, the RF-4C hooked to the tanker gives the impression of dangling from a pole.

As it happens, my host unit, the 380th Air Refueling Squadron, received the very last KC-135A delivered at Seattle on 12 January 1965. The KC-135 design (and the related but wholly different Boeing 707) has been the subject of many, many changes and conversions, so that the aircraft has appeared in more different variants than any other type ever to serve in US forces, but most of these changes took place after delivery. The Boeing production run of 820 airframes was limited to seven variants: 732 KC-135A tankers, 17 KC-135B tankers, 10 RC-135B reconnaissance aircraft, 15 C-135A transports, 30 C-135B transports, four RC-135A mapping and survey aircraft, and the 12 C-135F tanker/transports delivered to the French Air Force. The machine being piloted today by Capt Karen Cunningham came along towards the middle of the production run. Now almost a quarter of a century old, the basic airframe is almost certainly good for at least another 15 years of service.

At 29,000ft over New York State, Capt John Severski of the 49th Fighter-Interceptor Squadron eases his F-106A Delta Dagger up on to the boom of KC-135A tanker 58-0061. The F-106A is painted in a special scheme for the 1976 bicentennial of US independence. *New York ANG*

Above:
One of the Aeronautical Systems Division's many KC-135A test aircraft is 55-3135 (right), festooned with so many large windows that it was nicknamed the 'Piccolo Tube'. In this view, however, 55-3135 seems to be performing the tanker function, topping off the prototype Lockheed YC-141B Starlifter (66-0186). *Lockheed*

Having 'topped off' 'Zerox' flight and bade goodbye to the anchor orbit location known as 'William', the return flight to Mildenhall is routine. We encounter some turbulence and the airframe seems remarkably solid and steady. The approach over the wet slick East Anglia countryside is also routine. The KC-135 feels very solid underfoot, not easily disturbed by gusting. Cunningham makes a 'straight-in' approach with a rapid let-down and we are on the ground at Mildenhall. The crew heads for a debriefing, and I am handed a certificate for having flown a mission with a SAC combat crew.

The KC-135 transfers fuel three times as fast as the KC-97 Stratofreighter it replaced and does the job at the normal cruise speed of its receiver aircraft, making it an enormous improvement over the earlier machine. But the KC-135 was also designed for the secondary purpose of logistics support and cargo hauling, and has done yeoman service carrying people and things from place to place. Aerial refuelling equipment is all on the lower deck of the twin-lobed fuselage, leaving the upper deck clear for cargo or troop carrying. (Although both the flight cabin and the boomer's position aboard 'my' KC-135 were rather cramped, I was able to saunter freely around the entire upper fuselage in empty space which served no actual purpose on 'my' mission.) The aircraft can carry 80 passengers ('pax') or 50,000lb (22,600kg) of cargo, or a combination of both. Some bizarre cargoes have been reported aboard KC-135s at one time or another, including rattan furniture from the Philippines and cases of rich red wine from Sigonella, Italy. The stateside-based tankers which deploy temporarily to overseas locations like Mildenhall routinely carry whatever needs to be brought in that direction. It should be emphasised that it is the *tanker* KC-135 being discussed here, not the transport variant which has even greater load-carrying capacity.

It was as a tanker, of course, that the aircraft was conceived. And the design, development and operational and combat use of the Boeing KC-135 Stratotanker must be rated as one of the truly great stories in the annals of aviation.

The story begins long before 'my' mission in a KC-135, and is unlikely to be finished by the end of this century. In its beginnings, it is a story of vision on the part of Boeing people who saw the future and were willing to take a chance.

2 Test Ship

Boeing, that great builder of big American aircraft situated in the American northwest and synonymous with the city of Seattle, had an early beginning in the once-arcane art of air-to-air refuelling. As long ago as 1929 a Model 95 mailplane functioned as a receiver in tests, taking on gasoline from a Boeing Model 40-B which lowered a trailing hose to an aircrew member in the mailplane, who then inserted the hose's nozzle into the fuel tank filler pipe. No immediate result came from these trials, and in subsequent years Boeing became better known as a maker of bombers, the B-17 Flying Fortress and B-29 Superfortress leaving a mark on history which requires no comment. Incredibly, World War 2 saw American Marines seizing one Pacific island after another solely to bring bombers within striking range of Japan, and no one exploited air refuelling as a means to stretch those bombers' legs.

After VJ-Day it was not Boeing but a British firm, Flight Refuelling Ltd, which pioneered the hose-type refuelling system first employed on American B-29s and the 'probe and drogue' system widely employed from the 1940s onward, the latter being the US Navy's standard method today. With this system, of course, the receiver aircraft carries a 'probe', a long cylindrical tube, which fits snugly into the 'drogue', a funnel trailing by hose from the tanker, making it possible for the tanker to pump fuel into the recipient. (In fact gravity provides a significant boost.) 'Probe and drogue' remains one of the two predominant air refuelling systems in use in the world today and at present, in order to be compatible with US Navy receivers, the KC-135 has a secondary capacity to employ this method. But Boeing, the KC-135 and indeed air refuelling itself would be wholly different today were it not for the other predominant system, namely the 'flying boom'.

In November 1947 the newly-independent US Air Force was being run by the bomber generals, men like Curtis E. LeMay who had commanded the bombing campaigns against Germany and Japan and who believed in long-range airpower as the antidote to an increasingly unfriendly Soviet Union. The enormous clout wielded by men like LeMay spelled austere times for the fighter people who sought in vain for a larger slice of the budget pie to purchase an odd-looking machine called the F-86 Sabre, but these were heady days indeed for the Strategic Air Command (established on 21 March 1946), for bombers, and eventually for air refuelling.

SAC's global striking power was demonstrated on 2 March 1949 when B-50A Superfortress 46-010, *Lucky Lady II* of the 43rd Bomb Group, completed the first nonstop around-the-world

Below:
KC-135A Stratotanker 59-1511 lands at RAF Fairford, England, in 1985. *John Dunnell*

Described at the time as 'this hitherto classified device', Boeing's flying boom refuelling system was revealed publicly on 19 October 1949 on this KB-29P (former B-29A) Superfortress, 42-93921, seen in the insignia of the period with 'buzz number' BF-921. Boeing's first tanker was the KB-29M Superfortress, which employed a hose and reel method of refuelling. *USAF*

The US Air Force's second-generation tanker had been built by Boeing, but the conversion to the tanker role was carried out by Hayes Aircraft Corporation of Birmingham, Alabama, and the system employed was probe and drogue rather than Boeing's flying boom. Here Boeing KB-50J Superfortresses (formerly B-50D aircraft; 49-309 is in foreground) are seen at the Hayes facility in 1956. *Hayes*

flight, covering 23,452 miles (37,523km) in 94 hours, 1 minute. The crew of 14 commanded by Capt James Gallagher originated from and returned to Carswell AFB, Texas, and *Lucky Lady II* was refuelled four times in the air by KB-29M Superfortress tankers of the 43rd Air Refueling Squadron, which employed a hose system to transfer the fuel from tanker to receiver.

SAC was in the process of acquiring its own odd-looking hunk of machinery, the B-47 Stratojet which, like the Sabre, employed the dramatic new technology of swept wings. Eventually a most impressive force of 1,500 Stratojets carried the fires of the Cold War but how, then, were these bombers to attain the range needed to assault targets deep inside the Soviet Union? November 1947 was the month the Air Materiel Command (AMC) at Wright-Patterson AFB, Ohio, awarded Boeing a research contract which led over time to the 'flying boom' system and, later, to the KC-135.

The refuelling system on the KC-135 is similar in concept to that pioneered by Boeing on the KB-29, KB-50 and KC-97. It comprises a rigid boom that can be lowered and telescopically extended from the underside of the tanker and then 'flown' by the boom operator until the tip makes contact with a refuelling receptacle in the receiver aircraft that is formating behind and below the tanker. Fuel is pumped from the fuselage tanks through check valves, directly into the air refuelling manifold, to the air refuelling line valve, through the air refuelling pressure regulator and fuel flow transmitter, and then out through the boom. Some aircraft are equipped with a reverse-flow refuelling

system so that a receiver aircraft can assist the tanker should the latter be short of fuel itself.

All KC-135 aircraft have the familiar boom operator's station pod bulging beneath the rear fuselage. There is supposed to be space for a boom operator, an instructor and a student operator although the second and third members of this trio would have to sit flanking the boom operator with virtually no outside visibility. A pallet ('ironing board') with safety harnesses, intercom and oxygen equipment makes the boomer relatively comfortable. One set of boom operating controls is installed in the compartment, consisting of an instrument panel, boom hoist lever and boom telescope lever for use by the operator's left hand and a ruddevator control stick for use by the operator's right hand. A periscope can be used to broaden the operator's field of vision.

The refuelling boom consists of two concentric tubular sections capable of extending over a range of 24-27ft (8.5-14.3m). Nominal travel of the boom is in a cone within 30° left and right azimuth and an elevation of plus 12.5° and minus 50°. The boom is of course a telescoping rod (as distinguished from the hoses used in an earlier era), but because of its ruddevators which function as both rudders and elevators, the boom can indeed be 'flown' (guided) by boom operators like Sgt Baka. So for the remainder of this narrative the quotation marks will be removed: flying boom.

Early Tankers
While the hose-operated probe and drogue method was employed during the 1947-53 era by

Above left:
**Boeing KC-97G Stratofreighter
53-3816 was the last of 814 tankers
in this series delivered to the US
Air Force, all of them employing
the flying boom refuelling system.
Before the service career of these
fine aircraft ended, the KC-97L
variant was in operation with jet
engines under the wing (where fuel
tanks are seen here) to augment
piston power.** *Boeing*

Left:
**As late as 1975 this Missouri Air
National Guard KC-97L
Stratofreighter was refuelling F-4E
Phantoms of the 86th Tactical
Fighter Wing at Ramstein AB,
Germany. Even with jet
augmentation, the KC-97L had
difficulty maintaining the
minimum speed necessary for
effective refuelling of Phantoms.**
USAF

the US Air Force's 116 KB-29P and 136 KB-50J Superfortresses (as late as 1965 by KB-50J aeroplanes refurbished and upgraded by Hayes Aircraft Corporation of Birmingham, Alabama), Boeing shifted to the flying boom for its Model 367, or KC-97 Stratofreighter, and the first of 814 Seattle-built airframes in the KC-97 series entered service in 1951. The 306th Air Refueling Squadron at MacDill AFB, Florida (near Tampa) was the first unit to begin equipping with the KC-97. Its first aircraft, a KC-97E (51-183), was delivered on 14 July 1951, each SAC squadron being authorised 20 aircraft.

The long and successful contribution made by the KC-97 is often overlooked and some men who flew the KC-97 never loved any other aircraft as well, but a dilemma existed and it was unmistakable: combat aircraft, fighters and bombers, were pushed to speeds of around 600mph (960km/hr) by jet engines whilst combat support machines, including tankers, still strained along at a mere 350mph (560km/hr), pulled through the air by propellers. Struggling to link up with the flying boom lowered by a lumbering KC-97, the pilot of a B-47 Stratojet or F-101 Voodoo had to suck in his breath, throttle back, maintain a precarious angle of attack (AOA) and fidget mightily!

Boeing's management team saw the jet age coming and unilaterally funded the Model 367-80, better known as the Dash 80, at a cost of $1.6 million. Intended not only to function as a test ship for a faster tanker, more compatible with fast fighters and bombers, the Dash 80 was also to be the testbed for a first generation of American jet

airliners, to follow up on the obvious potential suggested by the de Havilland Comet and, later, the Tupolev Tu-104. This one-of-a-kind aircraft was referred to by the press, and even by Boeing's own house organ, as the Boeing 707, but it was not. In external appearance, however, the Model 367-80 was identical in appearance to the Boeing 707 civil airliner and the KC-135A tanker to follow. As a private venture, a risk, the consequences of which could not have been predicted for certain, the Dash 80 turned out to be a bold and successful move by Boeing and a milestone in the history of aviation.

The Model 367-80, with the evocative civil registration N70700, was rolled out on 14 May 1954 and soon embarked on an exhaustive, company-financed, proof-of-concept test programme. From then until now, one of the key roles of the basic Boeing design has been as a test ship — initially, for the purpose of its own development and proving, much later as the platform for a variety of experiments in advanced technology including today's 'Star Wars' research. By October 1956, as a part of the Boeing test programme, the Dash 80 was retrofitted with a flying boom for mid-air tanker coupling trials, but the US Air

Force shared Boeing's boldness and did not wait for proof that air-to-air refuelling by a jet tanker was practicable. With the onset of fiscal year 1955 (11 July 1954), the Air Force placed an initial order for 29 airframes in the KC-135A series, beginning with aircraft 55-3118.

Enter the KC-135A

Some myths die hard, and it is important at this juncture to dispel the notion that the KC-135A is somehow a military version of the Boeing 707 airliner. It is not. The KC-135A (or Boeing 717) *preceded*, and paved the way for, the commercial machine which became so successful with the world's civil carriers. Of course, both shared a common heritage in the vision of Boeing's engineers and finance people, and both are progeny of the private Model 367-80 prototype. The K-135A flew 18 months before the first genuine 707, however, and differs from it in several important respects, having a somewhat more narrow fuselage and entirely different cross-section, so that the two could not be produced on the same factory jigs. Throughout aviation history, given man's tendency to rank killing ahead of commerce, it has often happened that a technical breakthrough occurred first in the military area, only being applied to the civilian realm afterwards. So it was, in a sense, with the KC-135A.

Test Programme

While the prototype Dash 80 was still the only aircraft of its type actually flying, the US Air Force

Above:

Early in its flight-test programme the Boeing Model 367-80 was fitted with a flying boom refuelling device, seen here in the extended position. As used on production KC-135A Stratotankers, the telescoping, fuel-pressurised boom was 47ft (14.3m) in length and, in an emergency, was used in effect to tow an aircraft in trouble. *Boeing*

forged ahead, placing its *second* order for KC-135As. The 14 June 1956 edition of the manufacturer's *Boeing News* announced that the firm had been awarded a $145 million contract for additional KC-135As to be built at the Renton plant near Seattle. A fortuitous coincidence enabled the company to proceed with plans to roll out the first KC-135A on the same day, in the same ceremony, as the 814th and last KC-97.

Roll-out

The KC-135A saw the light of day officially during the week of 20 July 1956, when thousands at the Renton plant observed the roll-out of the last KC-97 (53-3616) and the first KC-135A (55-3118). The ceremony was accompanied by a low-level flyover of the Model 367-80 and of the company's other well-known product, a B-52 bomber. A predictable group of dignitaries was assembled for the occasion, including Boeing President William Allen, Air Force Lt-Gen C. S. Irvine (deputy chief of staff for materiel), Renton's Mayor Joseph R. Baxter, and Karen McGarrigle who had the distinction of being 'Miss Renton'. Miss McGarrigle christened 55-3118 *City of Renton*, although it was the mayor's wife who swung a bottle of cedar

water against metal for the event, assisted by Renton factory manager Harvey Kent. Twenty-one months and 13 days had transpired since the Air Force placed its first order for the KC-135A. The occasion, incidentally, came within three days of the 40th anniversary of the Boeing company.

Engineering ground tests of engines and pre-flight work on *City of Renton* began the week of 23 August 1956. Kent reported satisfactory progress with Boeing's 'shakedown', Air Force inspections and taxi runs, and indicated that the first eight production tankers would take off from Renton and land at Boeing Field in Seattle for delivery to the Air Force. The ninth airframe was to go to the nearby Moses Lake Flight Center for delivery. R. L. Loesch, project pilot on the KC-135 programme, told the press that the first nine production tankers would undergo an estimated 1,380 hours of flight testing, with one airframe to be subjected to three months of sub-zero investigations in simulated Arctic conditions in the climatic hangar at Eglin AFB, Florida. Aircraft 1, 2, and 3 were scheduled for flight testing by the company at Boeing Field while Aircraft 5 through 9 were scheduled for the Air Force at Edwards AFB, California; Loring AFB, Maine (an operational SAC base); Eglin; and a special adverse-weather testing location at Ladd AFB, Alaska.

Boeing's initiative in the jet market had established a momentum, and the pace was kept up. At the end of August 1956, Air Force Secretary Donald Quarles announced that the production of KC-135A Stratotankers would be speeded up, a previously-planned production rate of 20 per month to be realised 'substantially sooner' under Quarles's revised schedule. Gen Le-May, SAC commander, had told the Senate Armed Services Sub-committee of SAC's need for more jet tankers. Said LeMay, 'We [can] increase our intercontinental strike capability considerably from our planned base structure and with the same size bomber force if we [have] more jet tankers than we are now programmed to have'. Pointing out the obvious, LeMay compared the KC-135A to the piston-engine KC-97:

'The slower conventional tanker, in order to make proper contact with its [receiver] bomber, must depart [its base] several hours before the bomber. The bomber, forced to wait on the ground, is then exposed to enemy attack. The airplanes we are now refuelling are jet airplanes.

'A jet tanker has the same general performance characteristics as the bomber, and therefore can accompany the bomber, eliminating the rendez-vous problems. In addition, the performance of the jet tankers is such that the refuelling altitude is at a height above most of the weather . . . and adds to range because the bomber does not have to descend to piston-engine altitudes to receive its load of fuel'.

Left:
Roll-out ceremony. The Model 367-80 prototype leads a B-52 bomber in a flyover of the Boeing factory in Renton, Washington, as the final KC-97G and the first KC-135A are rolled out on the same day. *Boeing*

Right:
With Dix Loesch at the controls, aircraft 55-3118 *City of Renton* lifts off at Renton on 31 August 1956 for the first flight of a KC-135A Stratotanker. KC-97G tankers from the end of that type's production run are visible in background. *Boeing*

First Flight

Ten days ahead of schedule, just before 1pm on Friday 31 August 1956, 55-3118 *City of Renton* wheeled gracefully out on the taxiway at Renton, made a trial taxi run and took position at the south end of the runway for a historic maiden flight. Aboard were Boeing's colourful chief of flight test, A. M. (Tex) Johnston, and senior experimental test pilot R. L. (Dix) Loesch, the latter occupying the left-hand seat. Though Loesch was in command of 55-3118, Johnston ranked him and always seemed to attract more attention. Remarked company president William Allen:

'This is the first time Tex has made a first flight without his cowboy boots.' Loesch took the KC-135A aloft and after 1hr 19min landed at Boeing Field in Seattle. He later commented on the trouble-free flight: 'In the first place it was remarkable that the plane was in the air about a week and a half ahead of schedule and in the second place, it was my first time to fly a new-type airplane on its maiden flight'.

From the outset of its rigorous flight test programme it was apparent that the KC-135A had been designed to a standard of performance consistent with LeMay's high expectations. Powered by four Pratt & Whitney J57-P-39W turbojets which were as advanced as anything in their day (although the potential of the airframe outlived them, as will be seen in the re-engining programmes of the 1980s) and were rated at 13,750lb (6,237kg) thrust with water injection — the cause of the Stratotanker's sooty smoke trails — the KC-135A grossed 316,000lb (143,338kg). It was in every respect a heavier and more solid aircraft than its 707 civilian contemporary and thus needed a runway as long as 13,700ft (4,276m) in tropical weather, a distance which would have been unacceptable for the airliner.

The prototype in the series had a long life indeed; 55-3118 was still flying when this narrative was prepared in 1986. This machine and not a few others have exceeded 20,000 flight hours in spite of the severe wing bending which occurs at maximum weight, eloquent testimony to the toughness of the airframe. In the beginning the phenomenal success

of the Stratotanker seemed far from guaranteed, however. After three test flights and 3hr 38min in the air, *City of Renton* was temporarily laid up at Boeing Field for installation of additional equipment and flight test instrumentation. By October 1956 the KC-135A was flying again, and made its first successful delivery of fuel in flight, to a B-52. 'The KC-135 has had fewer systems problems than any plane I know of', Loesch was quoted.

Clearly not even Loesch could predict just how successful the KC-135A would be, but the flight test programme continued through the end of 1956 with so little difficulty that all scheduling goals were exceeded. On 24 January 1957 *City of Renton* was officially delivered to the US Air Force, Maj Erich Schleier signing its acceptance. A testing landmark of another kind was achieved the week of 7 February when a 50,000lb (22,600kg) KC-135A fuselage — devoid of wings or tail, and apparently not assigned a serial number — was trucked from Renton to Plant 1 in Seattle to be submerged in water for hydrostatic structural tests. By dousing the fuselage, then pressurising and depressurising it, engineers were able to calculate exact figures for the KC-135A's durability.

By 14 February 1957 the second KC-135A (55-3119) had already joined a flight test programme which had reached 124 flying hours and the third machine (55-3120) made its maiden jaunt from Renton to Seattle. Two months later the fourth machine (55-3121) was flown to Wright-Patterson AFB to begin weather testing which would take it to Eglin's climatic hangar, Alaska's cold and the Mojave Desert's heat. By now the number nine KC-135A (55-3126) had joined the flight test effort and had been christened *City of Moses Lake*, after the landmark where it landed after its first flight.

Production Underway

By June 1957, testing and deliveries of the KC-135A were proceeding so smoothly, with so little difficulty, that Boeing could get the aircraft into local newspapers only by trotting out another beauty queen — Margery Barr, who held the title Miss West Seattle — and posing her with it. Like many stories in aviation, the KC-135A was now a non-story. Newspapers and television carried reports when an aircraft splattered against a mountainside or disintegrated above a crowded city, *not* when a flight development and production effort proceeded with minimal difficulty.

Even at the end of June when the first three KC-135As to reach SAC were delivered to the 93rd Air Refueling Squadron, part of the 93rd Bomb Wing at Castle AFB, California (the first of these being 55-3127), the event was newsworthy only because of the presence of Col Winston Close, the Wing's deputy commander. Close, it seemed, had pulled off a hat trick. He had picked up the first B-29 manufactured by Boeing in Wichita in 1943 and the first B-52D in 1955.

In November 1957 a specially-equipped KC-135A named *Speckled Trout* took off from Boeing Field with a cargo of newsmen aboard for a flight to the east coast. It was one of the first occasions — during the same season that Sputnik became the world's first artificial satellite — when newsmen broadcast live reports from an aircraft in flight. *Trout* covered the almost 3,000 miles (4,800km) to Andrews AFB, near Washington DC, in 4hr 8min. The KC-135A was still not exactly news — Sputnik was — but it was now fully operational with the Strategic Air Command. Tests of various kinds would continue, but the basic issue was no longer in doubt: this was a service aircraft.

'If It Quacks . . .'

A rose is a rose, insisted poet Gertrude Stein, but when is a KC-135 a KC-135? While our purpose is to cover the KC-135 series, we have also included for convenience US military variants of the Boeing 707 airliner. Even without these, some 60-odd variants of our basic aircraft are flying around the globe today, depending on how you define a variant, so a KC-135 may not be a tanker at all but may be, instead, a transport, a command post or a reconnaissance aircraft. One of the KC-135's many roles is the test function, the subject of this chapter. Others are full-time or part-time duties which may or may not require the aircraft to be modified. Before moving ahead, then, it seems useful to remind the recognition buff what to look for on the pages which follow. Hence, these hints:

● *Look at the designation.* KC aircraft are usually tankers, but not always. C aircraft (for cargo) are *always* transports, not just usually, but some of the time VC aircraft are transports, too, used to carry dignitaries. EC aircraft have an electronic role of some sort and are usually flying command posts. RC aircraft have the reconnaissance role. Every machine in the KC-135 Stratotanker series has such a prefix, but machines derived from the Boeing 707 airliner have wholly different designations (E-3A, E-6A, EC-18B). The US Air Force's system for designating its aircraft dates to 1924 and is straightforward enough but it is far from perfect. To illustrate the inconsistencies, one test aircraft used by NASA for training its astronauts in zero-gravity flight was known as a C-135A transport (60-0378) while another test ship with the same role is simply a KC-135A tanker (59-1481).

● *Look at the fuselage.* A narrower double-lobe fuselage 128ft 10in (39.27m) long with very few windows identifies one of the many machines in the KC-135 series. A fuselage with larger diameter, full double-lobe cross-section, windows (sometimes) and greater length (sometimes *much* greater length) identifies a military derivative of the Boeing 707 airliner (E-3A, E-6A, EC-18B). Fuselage length of the airliner variants ranges from 138ft 10in (42.32m) for the Model 707-100 to 145ft 6in (44.35m) for the Model 707-300/400. The difference in fuselage diameter is a mere 4in (10cm), with the members of the smaller KC-135 family measuring an exact 12ft (3.66m) in diameter at the maximum.

Other external features peculiar to the KC-135 series and not found on derivatives of the Boeing

707 airliner include the plain pylon struts which support the engines (the 707 having some or all struts terminating in a ram air inlet for cabin, air-cycle conditioning) and, of course, the boom operator's position and high-speed refuelling boom pivoted under the rear fuselage.

● *Look at the engines.* All KC-135A tankers and some other members of the family are powered by the annular-intake Pratt & Whitney J57 (civil designation JT3C) two-spool, axial-flow turbojet engine with water injection which produces about 13,000lb (6,124kg) thrust at 8,200rpm and is notorious for smoky take-offs. Thrust reversers are not fitted. This engine weighs 3,870lb (1,755kg) and has a diameter of 38.90in (988mm). This is the same powerplant employed by the B-52 Strato-

Above:
The attractive lines of the KC-135A Stratotanker were evident from the beginning, witness this view of 55-3118 *City of Renton*, **the first aircraft in the series, on an early test flight.** *Boeing*

Below:
Boeing's Model 367-80, registered N70700, passes over the 55-3118 early in the latter's flight test programme. Production of Boeing's other major aircraft type, the B-52 (background), was shifted to Wichita to free the Renton plant for KC-135A manufacture. *Boeing*

fortress, which is perhaps the only warplane in inventory to make more smoke, and on the F-100 Super Sabre, F-101 Voodoo, F-102 Delta Dagger and F-8 Crusader fighters. By today's standard this engine is a far cry from state-of-the-art technology and appears small in overall dimensions.

All C-135B variants, all Boeing 707 derivatives (except the E-6A and Saudi KE-3A) and many rebuilds of the KC-135 series are powered by the Pratt & Whitney TF33 (civil designation JT3D) turbo-fan engine which produces about 18,000lb (8,164kg) thrust at 8,700rpm and was developed from the J57 through removal of the first three compressor stages and replacement by two fan stages, the result being a nacelle which is longer and more perfectly cylindrical in appearance. Thrust reversers are employed. This engine weighs from 4,130lb (1,873kg) to 4,570lb (2,073kg) with a diameter of 53.0in (1.34m). The turbofan was also

used on later B-52s and on the Lockheed C-141A Starlifter. The TF33 is far 'cleaner' and is newer, giving significantly better performance.

Newer KC-135R and French C-135FR aircraft employ the F108, known in civil use as CFM56-2B-1 and manufactured by CFM International, a consortium of General Electric and France's *Societe Nationale d'Étude et de Construction de Moteurs d'Aviation* (SNECMA). Saudi KE-3As and the E-6A will have the almost identical CFM56-2A-2. This engine weighs 4,612lb (2,092kg) and is 95.7in (2.43m) in length. A subsonic turbofan in the 20,000lb (9,060kg) thrust class, it is distinctly shorter and, more importantly, 'fatter' than other powerplants. It is no exaggeration to say that this engine on the KC-135R gives the illusion of dragging the ground, the simple result of its girth.

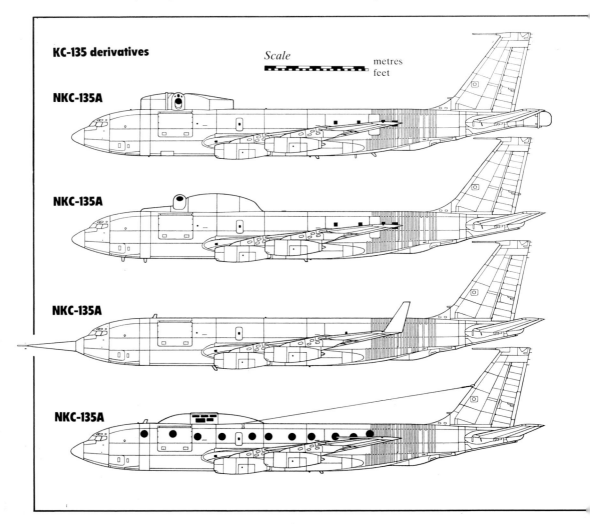

KC-135 derivatives

Scale

metres
feet

NKC-135A

NKC-135A

NKC-135A

NKC-135A

● *Look at the tail.* Early KC-135A tankers were delivered with a manually-operated rudder. These 'short-finned' aircraft had a height of 38ft 5in (11.71m) and were identifiable by the fin cap being mounted directly above the rudder. They were retrofitted, and later production KC-135s were delivered, with a powered rudder. This produced a 40in (1.02m) fin extension and is identified by a fin extension above the rudder with the fin cap installed on top, height of the aircraft being increased to 41ft 8in (12.7m).

The preceding hints will be of some help in sorting out the many kinds of KC-135 and related aircraft. Another way, of course, is to consider their roles. Again, in this work we consider that the many missions performed by the KC-135 family can be lumped into six broadly-defined roles — tanker, transport, reconnaissance, AWACS, command post and in this chapter, test.

Test Ship

Throughout the narrative which follows, we will make occasional use of a US Air Force report which bears the unwieldy and tongue-twisting title, *E/EC/KC/RC/WC-135 Aircraft Mission/Design/Series Report as of 1 July 85.* A mouthful indeed, this unclassified collection of paper is more often called simply the *Tinker Report*, after the name of the Air Force base in Oklahoma were it was prepared. Although now somewhat dated, the Tinker Report is the closest thing to a public order of battle for the KC-135 force which has been released. We shall be quoting from those items in the Tinker Report which provide listings of the current fleet of KC-135 tankers and their derivatives, and indicate some of the significant

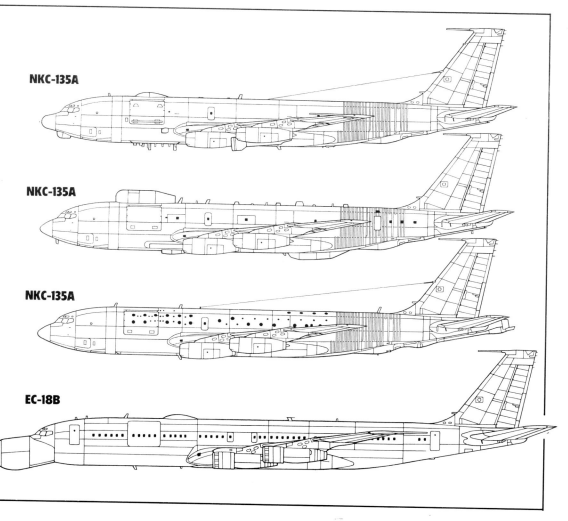

NKC-135A

NKC-135A

NKC-135A

EC-18B

changes to the fleet. To take, for example, the job of assisting in tests, our report lists three airframes in the C-135E series:

● **C-135E** is the designation for a trio of test aircraft associated with the Aeronautical Systems Division (ASD) at Wright-Patterson AFB, Ohio. The Tinker Report shows three in inventory as of 1 July 1985:

Serial No	Engine	Used by
60-372	TF33-PW-102	4950th TW/Wright-Patterson AFB, Ohio
60-375	TF33-PW-102	4950th TW/Wright-Patterson AFB, Ohio
60-376	TF33-PW-102	552nd AW&CW/Tinker AFB, Oklahoma

These were originally delivered as C-135A aircraft and were later in C-135N configuration before being converted to C-135E in 1982. Aircraft 60-372 and 60-375 were modified to EC-135N configuration for use in the Advanced Range Instrumented Aircraft (ARIA) programmes in earlier years. They were then modified and redesignated as C-135N in 1980. Aircraft 60-376 was reconfigured at Tinker AFB in 1972-73 to staff configuration. It was assigned to Military Airlift Command in 1975 and then to SAC in 1977, and currently operates at Tinker in support of the US Air Force's Space Command.

The preceding is a mouthful, too, but it introduces the bewildering array of designations by which various members of the KC-135 family are known. More than likely, a volume could be written about this trio of test C-135E aircraft alone. It was announced in October 1986 that the US Air Force and McDonnell Douglas would modify aircraft 60-372 to serve as a flying laser communications testbed under a $1.5 million, 42-month programme. Changes to 60-372 will include the installation of a 30in (0.9m) diameter optical window in the cargo door, an optical radome on top of the fuselage, a vibration-isolated mounting for optical hardware and microprocessing computing capability for automated data collection and in-flight analysis.

Although the ASD has been conducting airborne laser communications experiments since 1982, the conversion of 60-372 — which will introduce the new designation NC-135E — is to begin flying for this purpose in 1989, to design prototype laser communication systems for specific operational requirements. Previously the US Air Force had not had a permanent laser testbed and had to spend $250,000 to modify two aircraft each time laser tests were conducted.

The Test Role

Once the basic C-135 series airframe had graduated from its own test programme to full-fledged service as a TAC tanker, the US Air Force possessed a proven and versatile airframe ideally suited for a wide-ranging variety of experimental purposes. The ASD fleet at Wright-Patterson AFB, Ohio, already introduced, is perhaps the best known example of the C-135 series functioning as a test ship. In addition to the three aircraft already mentioned, eight more have been operated since the 1960s by ASD, which is itself a part of Air Force Systems Command (two of them on long-term lease to the US Navy).

NKC-135A is the designation applied to these aircraft, rebuilt for use as permanent test and research vehicles. The aforementioned Tinker Report lists them as follows:

Serial No	Engine	Used by
55-3119	J57-P-59	55th SRW/Offutt AFB, Nebraska
55-3120	J57-P-43	4950th TW/Wright-Patterson AFB, Ohio
55-3122/3124	J57-P-43	4950th TW/Wright-Patterson AFB, Ohio
55-3131/3132	J57-P-43	4950th TW/Wright-Patterson AFB, Ohio
55-3134	J57-P-43	US Navy/Douglas-Tulsa
56-3596	J57-P-43	US Navy/Douglas-Tulsa

The number of equipment items and missions tested with these airframes are too numerous even to mention briefly here. Aircraft 55-3123, for example, was used to test the Northrop A-LOTS (Airborne Lightweight Tracking System) which then became standard on the Stratotankers used in the Apollo project. A-LOTS is carried in a teardrop pod which hangs from the side of the aircraft. S/n 55-3123 was later temporarily configured in the role for which a permanent airframe has just been ordered, as an airborne laser laboratory for the Air Force Weapons Lab at Kirtland AFB, New Mexico. This happened before research in this field came to be viewed as part of the Reagan administration's Strategic Defense Initiative (SDI), popularly called Star Wars. The Apollo moon flight, followed by Star Wars, is heady stuff, yet this is only one example of the versatile Stratotanker's service as a test ship.

Each of the 11 NKC-135A aircraft, as noted, is different from the others. According to author Bill Gunston, some retain the short tailfin associated with early KC-135A airframes, which would make them unique among aircraft still flying today. S/n 55-3121, a member of the series prior to the

1 July 1985 date of the Tinker Report, was used to test the dorsal fence aerial array which found its way to the RC-135T reconnaissance aircraft. S/n 55-3123, as just mentioned, flew in several different configurations and with various dorsal protuberances in the HEL (high-energy laser) programme. S/n 55-3129 was fitted with a long nose probe and was used by NASA at the Dryden Flight Test Center, Edwards AFB, California, to evaluate the benefits that might be derived from the use of 9ft (2.74m) winglets installed on the wingtips. It was indeed found that fuel savings from the reduced lift-to-drag ratio provided with winglets would offset the cost of retrofitting winglets on a fleet-wide basis. First flight with the winglets was made on 24 July 1979 and as tests were conducted, a fuel saving of 8% was reported. In the early 1980s it was reported that a decision had been taken to retrofit the entire Stratotanker fleet with winglets, but as late as 1986 this had not been done, possibly because fuel savings were being achieved with re-engining programmes instead.

Another of the aircraft in this stable, 55-3132, is thought to have tested the giant cheek SLAR

Top:
One of the US Air Force's many test ships, Boeing KC-135A 55-3134 is seen at Wright-Patterson AFB, Ohio, on 15 May 1965. The aircraft had just acquired a huge bulge above its forward fuselage but retained its basic tanker configuration. This machine is thought to be depicted on delivery to the Aeronautical Systems Division (ASD) at Wright Field. *Clyde Gerdes*

Above:
Another example of the changes in the Stratotanker fleet is aircraft 60-376, originally built as a KC-135A tanker. Used by Air Force Systems Command for Airborne Astrographic Camera Testing, 60-376 was reconfigured in 1972-73 as a staff aircraft. Rebuilt with TF33-PW-102 turbofan engines in April-May 1982 and assigned as a staff aircraft to the 522nd Airborne Warning & Control Wing, the aircraft had been redesignated C-135E when seen in this June 1983 view. *Paul Bennett*

(Sideways-Looking Airborne Radar) installation which later became a feature of several reconnaissance machines in the separate RC-135 series. Aircraft 55-3134 and 56-3596 (said, erroneously, in one report on Boeing's remarkable machine, to be

Above:
**Typical of the stable of test aircraft at the USAF's
Aeronautical Systems Division (ASD), Wright-Patterson
AFB, Ohio, is this NKC-135A (55-3132). In an earlier
configuration the aircraft was a testbed for sideways-
looking airborne radar (SLAR). As seen here, it was used
for the 'Big Crow' missile vulnerability programme, with
large canoe fairings on the fuselage. This view on landing
approach was taken in May 1982.** *Paul Bennett*

different numbers for the same airframe) were
transferred to the US Navy and are maintained by
McDonnell Douglas/Tulsa, Oklahoma, under US
Navy contract. The Tinker Report states that these
aircraft 'have been modified to perform ECM/
ECCM (electronic countermeasures/electronic
counter-countermeasures) missions and may differ
from Air Force aircraft in electronics equipment
and installation location'. With regard to the entire
group of NKC-135A machines, the 1 July 1985
report says: 'These aircraft [the 11 NKC-135As]
perform such roles as countermeasures testing,
airborne laser laboratory testing, water spray
testing to simulate rain and icing conditions,
satellite vulnerability testing, refuelling boom
testing, reconnaissance strike equipment testing
and weightlessness testing'.

On 3 August 1979 the author was given a tour of
ASD at Wright-Patterson and had a good,
first-hand look at many of the aircraft in this test
stable. While outwardly not quite as impressive as
the long-nosed ARIA aircraft (*Apollo*, and later
Advanced Range Instrumented Aircraft, or flying
tracking stations, to be discussed just below), each
NKC-135A test machine was truly one of a kind,
completely different from all of the others. Pilots
and crews alike point out that the aircraft in the
C-135 series are ideal for testing just about
anything at contemporary jet speeds and performance regimes.

It has long been rumoured, though never
confirmed, that the Air Force even considered
using the C-135 as a gunship! The aerial gunship
concept, which calls for using sideways-aiming
ordnance to be fired at ground targets by an
aircraft making pylon turns around a stationary
point, was proven in Vietnam. In the conflict
there, AC-47, AC-119 and AC-130 gunships
employed a wide range of ordnance, everything
from miniguns to 105mm howitzers, against
ground targets. At least one additional aircraft
type, the Convair C-131, was tested for the
gunship role. While prop-driven engines and high
wings seemed best for this mission, the jet-
powered, low-wing C-135 was at least considered.

Flying Tracking Stations
EC-135N was one of the designations given to
rebuilt tankers used as ARIA aircraft and
recognised by gigantic, bulbous nose radomes
housing 85in (2.16m) parabolic dish scanners.
Some of these aircraft were also fitted with
A-LOTS. By the time of the 1 July 1985 report
summarising the US Air Force's Stratotanker fleet,
their designation had been changed to the
following:

EC-135E was the appellation for the ARIA *after*
conversion to TF33-PW-102 turbofan engines. As
of 1 July 1985, the EC-135E forced totalled four
airframes, namely:

Serial No	Engine	Used by
60-374	TF33-PW-102	4950th TW/Wright-Patterson AFB, Ohio
61-326	TF33-PW-102	4950th TW/Wright-Patterson AFB, Ohio
61-329	TF33-PW-102	4950th TW/Wright-Patterson AFB, Ohio
61-330	TF33-PW-102	4950th TW/Wright-Patterson AFB, Ohio

As the report says:

'Originally, these aircraft were delivered as C-135A aircraft. They were modified to EC-135Ns and then converted to EC-135Es when the J57 engines were replaced.

'These aircraft were modified to support the Apollo and Eastern Test Range/Western Test Range (ETR/WTR) programs. Special equipment includes UHF, VHF and HF transmitters and receivers, timing equipment, displays and consoles to monitor operations and equipment for optical and instrument checkout. After the completion of the Apollo program, the aircraft were redesignated as Advanced Range Instrumented Aircraft [in order to] retain the ARIA acronym.'

It might be added that ARIA aircraft served, in effect, as diplomats. During the Apollo spaceflight programme, which culminated in the 21 July 1969 moon landing by the Apollo 11 lunar module, NASA's worldwide network of ground tracking stations (in locations as remote as Ivato, Madagascar) was backed up by the peripatetic ARIA Stratotankers. They literally girdled the globe.

As will be seen throughout the pages that follow, other members of the C-135 family are used for various others purposes which fall in the general category of test operations. One of the C-135A transports, for example, s/n 60-377, has been operated by ASD as a laser communications testbed. One of the C-135C transports (61-2669) is actually employed as an avionics testbed. Numerous other Stratotankers have been employed in a variety of other experimental programmes.

Every major American aircraft type has been dragged out on to the high wooden trestle at Kirtland AFB, New Mexico, far from any external contact with metal, to determine the type's susceptibility to EMP, or electro-magnetic pulse, the crippling electrical shock waves from a high-megaton nuclear explosion. The effects of

EMP on the C-135 series is especially important to defence planning because so many members of the C-135 family function as airborne command posts, carrying the generals and battle staff who will continue a nuclear conflict if ground command centres are lost. In the case of those EMP tests at Kirtland, the C-135 performed a test role without leaving the ground!

The preceding discussion of the test role is, of course, only a glimpse at a very large story. Given its practical utility and versatility, the C-135 will undoubtedly be used for many more test functions. To quote John R. Eddington, a propulsion technician assigned to Stratotanker support work at Tinker AFB, Oklahoma, 'The basic airframe has so many possibilities, it would be easier to think of some kind of experiment that has *not* been tried with one of the C-135 airplanes.'

Boeing 707 Derivatives
Those flying tracking stations, the ARIA aircraft, were such a success with the moon-landing programme and later with other space shots that the Air Force badly wanted more. Nearly three decades after the first flight of the first KC-135, ASD planners at Wright Field asked for more and were told that KC-135s were too badly needed elsewhere for any more to be spared. Apparently, with reluctance, ASD planners realised that they would have to acquire used 707 airliners and convert them if new ARIA aircraft were to be obtained. ASD made arrangements for the purchase of eight former American Airlines

Right:
Turbofan-powered C-135B 61-2662 was an ASD electronic systems testbed when seen during this visit to RAF Mildenhall, England, in 1978. Later, this airframe was converted to RC-135S standard for the reconnaissance role. *Paul Bennett*

Below right:
Yet another example of a multi-faceted test Stratotanker, 62-4128 was delivered as a C-135B, was modified into a Telemetry Range Instrument aircraft for work in the space programme, and later acquired the Advanced Range Instrumented Aircraft (ARIA) configuration seen here, with its unusual long nose. In 1985 this airframe was undergoing reconfiguration to become an RC-135X reconnaissance aircraft. *Via Robert F. Dorr*

Boeing 707-320Cs which were initially given the Air Force designation C-18A before modification. These aircraft received serials 81-0891/0898, having been formerly on the civil register as N7598A, N7567A, N7569A, N8403, N7566A, N8401, N7563A and N7565A. Like all airliners of this type, these aircraft were 18ft (5.48m) longer than members of the C-135 family and had windows not found on C-135s.

Once modified for the ARIA role with the characteristic long proboscis associated with that mission, these aircraft acquired the designation EC-18B. Their extra fuselage space permitted improvements to the overall mission capability with the fitment of a Sonobuoy Missile Impact Location System (SMILS) to pinpoint test missile impact at proving grounds. In addition to the scoring-capability SMILS, the Optics & Meteorological Systems provide data on the re-entry of space vehicles as they penetrate the earth's atmosphere. These two modifications were carried out by E-Systems Inc at Greenville, Texas.

On 12 January 1986 an EC-18B moved to a pre-positioned location near Nairobi, Kenya, to begin aerial tracking of a RCA communications satellite launched from the Space Shuttle *Colum-bia*. This marked the first operational mission by an EC-18B, specifically by aircraft 81-0891 assigned to ASD's well-known 4950th Test Wing. The EC-18B was delivered to the wing in January 1985 and spent most of that year being prepared for operational service. Final evaluation of internal electronic systems was performed on 7 December 1985 when the EC-18B flew a missile re-entry tracking mission alongside one of ASD's ARIA EC-135Es. Telemetry data collected and recorded by the EC-18B compared consistently with that obtained by the proven EC-135.

Of the eight airliners acquired by ASD, it appears that four were initially to be converted to the ARIA role with the others retaining their passenger-carrying duties for some time to come. The modification process which produces a space-tracking aircraft involves two years of intensive work including the fitment of the now-familiar bulbous nose which houses a 9ft airborne steerable antenna radome used for precision telemetry reception. Internally, each EC-18B is equipped with a navigation station, cockpit avionics compatible with the mission, telemetry recording equipment and accommodation for up to 24 people.

3 Transport

In my transit apartment in Seoul, the phone rang. 'They're putting you on', a guy at the embassy told me. I would return to Washington from a two-month Korean TDY (temporary duty) stint not by commercial airliner but aboard a Boeing VC-135B Stratolifter of the 89th Military Airlift Wing. I was hitching a ride, so to speak, albeit as an official traveller. The purpose of the flight was to carry Ambassador William J. Porter and our field commander in Korea, Gen John Michaelis, to congressional hearings in Washington. It was 5 June 1971.

The V prefix originally meant administrative aircraft. In recent years it has become synonymous with the term VIP, for very important person, the 89th Wing being the US Air Force's specialist in hauling dignitaries from one end of the planet to the other. My VC-135B was a genuine member of the Stratotanker family even if not all of the transports operated by the 89th MAW were. Beginning with the President of the United States and including the Vice-President, Secretary of State, members of Congress and many others, the 89th MAW, based at Andrews AFB, Maryland (just outside the capital), had an impressive roster of passengers and often carried them on that *other* Boeing aircraft. Perhaps the saddest mission ever carried out by the wing was the job of returning John F. Kennedy from Dallas on 23 November 1963.

Boeing 707 Variants

The aircraft used on *that* day, like many of the jet transports used by the wing, was not a KC-135A Stratotanker in any form. The presidential aircraft, Air Force One, was a militarised Boeing 707 given the USAF designation C-137. Like several Boeing 707 derivatives in this narrative (C-18, E-3, E-6), the C-137 is included even though it is a different aircraft type.

Before the jet age, American presidents had flown in a variety of piston-driven VIP transports. President Roosevelt, during World War 2, had flown in a B-24 Liberator and a C-54 Skymaster, the latter nicknamed *Sacred Cow*. President Truman, who held office until 1953, had a VC-118B, a military version of the Douglas DC-6, known as *Independence*. President Eisenhower travelled abroad in a Lockheed C-121A Constellation (48-610), named *Columbine*, and before leaving office on 20 January 1961, Ike also became the first president to fly in the Boeing VC-137A.

The first of these military Boeing 707s was a Model 707-153, designated VC-137A, configured with a 22-seat VIP interior and delivered on 4 May 1959 to the 1289th Air Transport Squadron. This unit belonged to the 1254th Air Transport Wing, which at the time was the major flying unit of Headquarters Command; this wing was reorganised as the 89th Military Airlift Wing during January 1966 and absorbed into Military

Above:
In the mid-1980s the USAF's Aeronautical Systems Division acquired several used, turbofan-powered Boeing 707 airframes. Wholly different in appearance from the KC-135 series, as evident from the many windows, these aircraft were given the designation C-18A. C-18A 81-0895 is seen taxiing at RAF Mildenhall, England, in July 1986. *Paul Bennett*

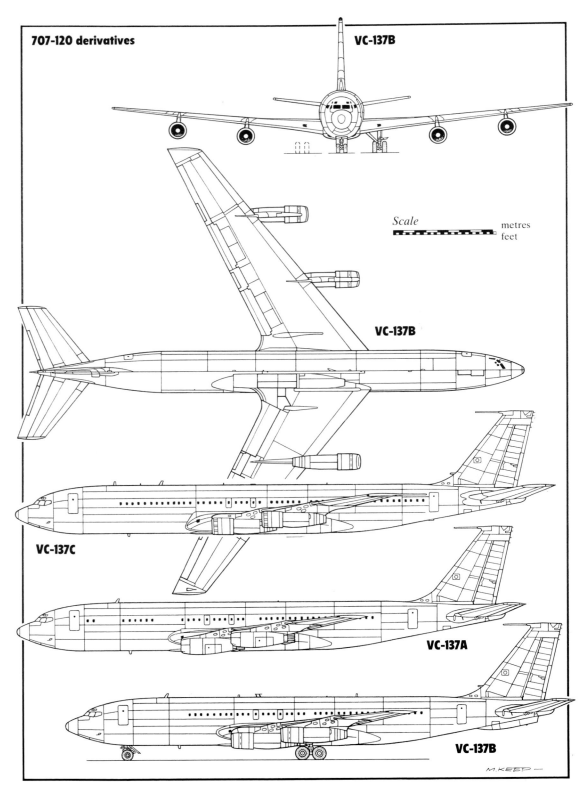

707-120 derivatives

VC-137B

VC-137B

Scale metres feet

VC-137B

VC-137C

VC-137A

VC-137B

M. KEEP —

Airlift Command with the demise of Headquarters Command.

The three VC-137A aircraft (58-6970/6972) were powered by 13,750lb (6,237kg) thrust Pratt & Whitney JT3C engines, each fitted with a large noise-suppression nozzle with 20 separate tubes. Because these were 'water-burning' engines, meaning that their power was boosted by water injection, they soon became covered with soot from wet takeoffs, when not only noise but black smoke were emitted on an impressive scale. Later, the three VIP transports were redesignated VC-137B when retrofitted with 18,000lb (8,164kg) thrust Pratt & Whitney JT3D turbofans, the civilian equivalent of the TF33 powerplant.

An additional aircraft in the series was delivered in October 1962. VC-137C, s/n 62-6000, was used regularly as the President's machine, including that awful day in Dallas.

In October 1973 the Air Force One mission was taken over by yet a further machine in the series, a newly-purchased military Boeing 707-353B, also designated VC-137C and given serial 72-7000. Also powered by JT3D engines, this second VC-137 had special communications equipment enabling the president to be in contact with US diplomatic and military centres in all parts of the world. During the Carter administration the V prefix was dropped, leaving the 89th MAW with three C-137B and two C-137C aircraft.

Two new USAF serials, 85-6973/6974, have been allocated to E Systems Inc in Dallas for the conversion of two additional 707 airliners to C-137C standard. These two VIP transports were expected to be delivered in 1987. Thus, if a table were constructed like those used elsewhere in this narrative, it would show:

Serial No	Engine	Used by
*58-6970/6972	JT3D	89th MAW/Andrews AFB, Maryland
62-6000	JT3D	89th MAW/Andrews AFB, Maryland
72-7000	JT3D	89th MAW/Andrews AFB, Maryland
85-6973/6974	JT3D	89th MAW/Andrews AFB, Maryland

Other variants of the Boeing 707 airliner were delivered to Canada and Iran with in-flight refuelling capability using wingtip hose wheels and drogues. Boeing has operated a demonstrator in this configuration, showing it as recently as the 1984 Farnborough Air Show, in the hope of obtaining additional orders. Since the Iranian revolution, the Islamic Republic of Iran Air Force (IRIAF) has been struggling to keep its Boeing 707-3J9C in flyable condition, to refuel F-4 and

F-14 fighters. Again it must be said that because the 707 is a different airframe, these military aircraft are *not* part of the KC-135 Stratotanker story, but they *do* demonstrate the versatility and durability of the basic Boeing concept.

In very recent years, plans have been advanced to replace the 89th MAW's presidential aircraft with a larger machine such as a Boeing 747. The pending delivery of two new C-137s seems to put this step farther away.

Flying the Transport

My own flight in a VIP transport reflected the decision of the US Air Force to acquire machines which *were* a part of the KC-135 series. The Military Air Transport Service (MATS), which soon afterward was rechristened Military Airlift Command (MAC), purchased 18 C-135A cargo/troop transports (60-369/378; 61-326/330; and three conversions from KC-135A tankers, these being 60-356/357 and 60-360) and dubbed them Stratolifter since they did not perform the tanker function. These were known to the company as the Model 717-157 and powered by 'water-burning' J57-59W engines, all but the three conversions also having the taller vertical tail fin which was associated with the series from midway through its production run.

These were followed in MATS/MAC service by the C-135B baseline fan-engined transport, the company Model 717-158, with TF33-5 turbofan engines, these machines being equipped with a refuelling boom operator's position in addition to the 'airline style' interior, but not having the actual boom. Thirty aircraft were produced with the C-135B designation (60-331/332; 61-2662/2674; 62-4125/4139). The C-135B first flew on 15 February 1962. The Boeing transports would eventually become redundant when the Lockheed C-141A Starlifter joined the Military Airlift Command fleet, and most of them were later converted to other missions, but for many years they transported people and supplies to every corner of the globe.

The US Air Force's unclassified 1 July 1985 report will now be quoted on the transport variants.

● **C-135A** was, as indicated, the first transport version, consisting of three conversions and 15 new airframes. As of the date of the report, only two machines were still flying with the C-135A designation, as indicated below:

Serial No	Engine	Used by
60-377	J57-43	4950th TW/Wright-Patterson AFB, Ohio
60-378	J57-59	55th SW/Offutt AFB, Nebraska

60-377 was modified by Air Force Systems Command to perform various research and development missions, and by 1 July 1965 the aircraft was configured as a LASERCOM (laser communications) testbed aircraft. We have already discussed this function elsewhere.

Aircraft 60-378 had earlier been modified by the command for use by NASA (National Aeronautics & Space Administration) to conduct 'zero-G' astronaut training. The aircraft was removed from those duties and assigned to SAC in 1977 as an administrative support aircraft, a kind of very large 'hack' primarily for the personal use of the SAC commander. The first of the two airframes, clearly, belongs more appropriately in the section on test ships (Chapter 2) while the second is a present-day transport.

● **C-135B**, again as has already been noted, was the designation for the turbofan-powered transport in the series, 30 of which were delivered to the Military Air Transport Service between January and August 1962. Because their powerplant was more efficient than the water-injection engines found on many of the early tankers, it was perhaps inevitable that these airframes would be chosen for modification to special roles. By the time of the report being used as a basic source here, only five aircraft were still flying in active inventory with this designation as follows:

Serial No	Engine	Used by
62-4125	TF33-P-5	435th TAW/Ramstein AB, Germany
62-4126	TF33-P-5	89th MAW/Andrews AFB, Maryland
62-4127	TF33-P-5	89th MAW/Andrews AFB, Maryland
62-4129	TF33-P-5	89th MAW/Andrews AFB, Maryland
62-4130	TF33-P-5	89th MAW/Andrews AFB, Maryland

The Air Force report notes that aircraft 62-4129 and 62-4130 were configured from the C-135B passenger/cargo configuration to what is called a Special Air Mission (SAM) configuration, this being the term for a VIP transport. This happened in 1967, when airline-style interiors were installed. The other three aircraft were configured to the SAM requirement in 1968. As the reader will soon see, 62-4129 was the aircraft in which the author made a protracted flight.

● **C-135C** is the designation for three further airframes which properly deserve to be treated in the transport section on Stratotanker variants. This series is unique in that the aircraft are fitted with an air refuelling receiver system which

enables them to take on fuel from tankers, thereby increasing their range and endurance. These machines were originally delivered as C-135Bs and were modified to the WC-135B weather-reconnaissance mission in 1965. Aircraft 61-2668 and 61-2669 were modified to staff configuration in 1973; 61-2669 was further modified in 1975 to its present configuration, which is identified by the term 'Pacer Speckled Trout'. Aircraft 61-2671 was modified to operational staff support configuration in 1974, completing the trio:

Serial No	Engine	Used by
61-2668	TF33-P-5	Det 1, 89th MAW/Hickam AFB, Hawaii
61-2669	TF33-P-5	Det 1, 4950th TW/Andrews AFB, Maryland
61-2671	TF33-P-5	Det 1, 89th MAW/Hickam AFB, Hawaii

And just what is a 'Pacer Speckled Trout'? The Tinker Report, source of our material on current-inventory listings, explains that 61-2669 is used by Air Force Systems Command as an avionics testbed aircraft. However, all three airframes are also listed as providing mission support and it is clear that their primary role is as transports rather than test ships.

Transport History
The C-135 transport made its maiden flight on 19 May 1961 and initial deliveries to the MATS Terminal at McGuire AFB, New Jersey, commenced in July 1961. A press release from the period credited the C-135B with being able to carry 89,000lb (40,117kg) of cargo or 126 fully equipped combat troops or 54 ambulatory patients with medical attendants. The role of hospital plane was soon taken over by the Douglas C-9A Skytrain but during its brief period as a transporter of those needing medical help, the C-135B performed admirably. Included among possible combat cargo loads were 376 boxes of ammunition or 1,090 cases of 'C' rations.

Top left:
One of 30 turbofan-powered aircraft delivered to the Military Airlift Command as the C-135B Stratolifter, 62-4128 is seen with its wide cargo door open at McGuire AFB, New Jersey, on 20 May 1967. Although employing the basic KC-135A fuselage, these transports did not have refuelling systems or refuelling booms.
Roger F. Besecker

Left:
With a later paint scheme than the one shown in the previous view, VC-137B 58-6972 is seen again at its Andrews AFB home base. *USAF*

45

On 17/18 April 1962 Maj Dave Crow flew a C-135B to a new payload-to-height record by lifting 66,139lb (29,950kg) to a height of 47,170ft (14,369m), while Maj Robert Hamann's crew established the payload-speed record carrying a 30,000kg load around a 2,000km course at a speed of 616mph (985.60km/hr).

C-135 Stratolifter transports soon began to appear around the world. Sadly they were involved in two major air disasters. First, 75 people were killed when C-135B 61-0322 crashed at Clark Air Base in the Philippines on 11 May 1964. Then, 25 June 1965, no fewer than 85 people lost their lives when C-135A 60-0373 was lost at Los Angeles International Airport, California. Despite these blemishes, the type has had a remarkably good safety record and has accumulated millions of miles of flying. One eventless flight, to return to the VIP transport role, was the 'special air mission' which carried the author.

Into the Mission
On 5 June 1971 an embassy car took me from downtown Seoul to outlying Kimpo International Airport (once known as K-14) to board Boeing VC-135B (as the aircraft was designated at that time) Stratolifter 62-4129 of the 89th Military Airlift Wing. At the time a crew member told me that 62-4129 was a converted tanker. He was wrong. As soon became clear, the aircraft was in fact never a tanker at all, although as a transport it has great fuel capacity.

VIP passenger John Michaelis, the four-star general who wore two hats as commander of US forces and of the United Nations Command in Korea, had never been a patient man. During World War 2 he had been decorated at Anzio; in Korea, he'd led parachute assaults against the enemy. Now they wanted him on the Hill, as the location of the US Congress was called, and Michaelis was going to get there the fastest way. As I went aboard, one of several mess attendants in spiffy, bright-coloured coveralls told me that the aircraft could easily fly non-stop from Kimpo to Andrews AFB just outside Washington, a distance rather more than halfway around the world. On this trip, however, we would make a fuel stop at Elmendorf AFB, Alaska — which lay directly on the way — because Gen Michaelis liked the food at the officers' club there!

Above:
An early view of a C-135B Stratolifter with TF33 turbofan engines shows the Military Air Transport Service (MATS) markings. Shortly after acquisition of the C-135B, this user changed its name to Military Airlift Command (MAC). *Robert F. Dorr*

Right:
VC-135B Stratolifter 62-4129 was the aircraft on which the author flew as a passenger from Kimpo AB, Korea, to Andrews AFB, Maryland, on 5 June 1971. The aircraft is operated as a VIP transport by the 89th Military Airlift Wing. *USAF*

I was invited to make myself comfortable in a part of the VC-135B Stratolifter which had seats for 16 people, in groups of four divided into pairs, facing each other across tables. It felt more like a first-class railroad car than a jet transport. The 16-seat portion of the VC-135B occupied a space which would surely have held a hundred people on an ordinary jetliner. Yet even this was crowded compared to the plush area, farther forward, where Gen Michaelis and Ambassador Porter occupied accommodations intended for *six* people filling nearly half the interior of the fuselage!

We made the very long take-off roll associated with the type, and climbed at a very sharp angle with the front-cabin crew aware that we were only 33 miles (52.8km) south of heavily-fortified North Korean gun positions. In fact, although the North Koreans had not shot down a friendly aircraft in two years — not since 15 April 1969, when two MiG-17s downed a US Navy Lockheed EC-121K Warning Star over the Sea of Japan, killing all 31 aboard — taking off from Kimpo was not exactly a low-risk experience. Only a few weeks earlier, itchy trigger fingers belonging to *South* Korean gunners had sent a spray of shells hurling around a Northwest Airlines jetliner taking the same route that we were following today. It was, therefore, a comfort to see the gnarled hills and terraced paddy fields of Korea fall behind as the VC-135B climbed out over the sea.

I was heading home. Back in Washington were a wife and a 12-week-old firstborn son whom I had not seen since 11 weeks ago. I settled back into the plush, cushioned seat of the VC-135B, stayed out of a card game being played by my three seatmates — other US government employees for whom space had been available — and enjoyed the throb of the engines. Those of us who spend all of our time around aircraft often cannot see the forest for the trees, so we forget what aviation is all about. A faster, easier way home is what aviation is about.

Years earlier, in uniform, stranded at Chicago's O'Hare Airport, I'd lacked by a dollar or two the ticket fee to get aboard a flight that would take me home for Christmas. A young Navy guy, seeing me in my Air Force uniform, crestfallen at being a dollar short, had handed me the cash I needed. 'Help out a sailor some time, buddy'. In cold and snow, I clambered aboard the Vickers Viscount belonging to Capital Airlines which took me to Washington, and I've been returning to Washington ever since. Flying home is what aviation is about.

Look at a globe. Draw an imaginary line from Seoul, Korea, to Washington DC. Imagine a jet transport which can routinely cover that distance non-stop.

As I soon learned from Gen Michaelis himself — he came walking back through the cabin, wearing expensive tweed coveralls and loose slippers, both designed for wear solely whilst flying in this aircraft — the decision to make a stop had more to do with winds and navigational factors than with the size of the T-bone steaks in the Chateau at Elmendorf. The 89th MAW flight crew of the VC-135B had decided that, because of headwinds, it would be prudent to pause at Elmendorf before pressing on to Washington. The big Boeing set down after a half-night, with the first pink cracks of sunrise breaking over the Alaskan airbase. The Kimpo-Elmendorf leg was just over nine hours, exactly half in daylight, half in darkness, with dawn coming after an artificially brief night. Crew members of the 89th MAW use various tricks to adjust their bodies and minds to time-zone changes — they recommend brief catnaps, frequent small meals, and plenty of water — but in truth, there really is no way to cope with jet lag. You simply suffer through.

On to Washington

The Chateau, as the field-grade officers' mess at Elmendorf was named, proved to offer a sumptuous repasse indeed. Breakfast included eggs and an 18-ounce steak. Once we got into the air for the second leg, however, the next meal turned out to be every bit as succulent as the one we'd had on the ground. Grilled fillet of sole, tartar sauce, Plymouth spinach, string potatoes, a dry white wine. On a typical 'special air mission' with a VIP aboard, the VC-135B carries a chef and the cuisine can be tailored to the wishes of the principal passenger; in what seemed an odd reversal, Henry Kissinger was said to prefer a bland American selection of meat and potatoes while Richard Nixon savoured more esoteric continental dishes. The flight attendants (all men in 1971) are rigorously trained in catering to passengers' needs. The flight attendants must be prepared for anything. An Army colonel often travelling to Saigon on White House missions, Alexander Haig kept trying to stop smoking via the expedient of never carrying any cigarettes, yet he frequently wanted to light up and wanted his brand, so a supply of Salems was kept just out of his reach. John Connally, Secretary of the Treasury, was always asking to know the exact latitude and longitude of the aircraft in flight, as well as other geographical details. ('Adak, Alaska? How far is that from Houston?') At one time or another, the VC-135B flight attendants served as shoeshine boys, wine stewards, telephone operators and first-aid attendants. Of course, all are trained in emergency procedures although no VIP flight has ever suffered a serious accident.

The VIP transport role is emphasised here because, over the years, this has increasingly

Below:
VC-135B Stratolifter 62-4125, with turbofan engines, almost no windows and no refuelling boom, is used for VIP flights by the Military Airlift Command's 89th Wing at Andrews AFB, Maryland. With a non-standard serial number presentation on its tail, the aircraft is seen at RAF Mildenhall, England, in June 1983. *Paul Bennett*

become the principal mission of the Military Airlift Command's Boeings. The much more routine job of ferrying troops, vehicles and supplies around the world has been increasingly performed by civilian airlines operating under contract. The 1986 crash of a 'stretched' DC-8 carrying peacekeeping troops home from the Middle East, a blow which crippled the US Army's 101st Airborne Division, has caused the use of charter flights to come under intense scrutiny, but even if the job were returned to the Air Force, it would probably be handled by Lockheed aircraft, namely the C-141B and C-5B.

My trip aboard VC-135B 62-4129 was smooth and easy, even though the eight-hour leg from Elmendorf to Andrews brought the total flying time to a wearying 17 hours. As we bore down over Canada towards the American east coast, the flight crew introduced themselves briefly. Pilot and aircraft commander Lt-Col Edwin Horney had flown KC-135A tankers in South-East Asia before shifting to the VIP transport. As a rule, however, tanker pilots remain in SAC while transport pilots tend to pass their careers in the Military Airlift Command. The flight crews responsible for the lives of Washington policymakers tend to be more mature, more experienced, and higher ranked than 'ordinary' transport pilots. All seem to have universal praise for the VIP-carrying variants of the Boeing KC-135, although they might well have been equally enthusiastic had the Convair CV-880 or Douglas DC-8 been chosen instead.

With my VC-135 flight more than 15 years in the past, the business of ferrying VIPs today has taken on new twists. Now, not merely the flight attendants but the pilots are often women. (Women make up about 16% of the US armed forces, which abolished separate women's arms such as the WAC and WAF and fully integrated female members shortly after conscription ended and an all-volunteer force was launched in 1974.) During the austere years of the Carter administration, the V prefix in the aircraft designation was regarded as ostentatious so the aircraft became, simply, C-135B and C-137C. By that time the VC-137A and VC-137B aircraft had been upgraded to C-137C standard.

Sad Duty

Lyndon B. Johnson remains the only president ever sworn-in aboard a Boeing transport or, for that matter, any other aircraft. That happened on 22 November 1963, within two hours of President Kennedy's assassination, and the ceremony took place with Jacqueline Kennedy aboard Air Force One at Johnson's side, her skirt still bloodstained. The changing times may not have brought any sadder moment, but in more recent years the sad moments seem to be coming more frequently. Fortunately, happier events have occurred as well.

The individual whims of a new generation of leaders now challenge a new generation of 'special air mission' chefs, flight attendants and flight crews. During the early days of the 1982 Falklands war, even the 89th MAW with its vast fleet of Boeings and other aircraft was sorely tasked as Alexander Haig — no longer a colonel now, but Secretary of State, and still trying to stop smoking — jaunted between London and Buenos Aires. At one point Haig made three flights in a day. Shuttle diplomacy means only one thing to the Boeing transport crews — hard work.

Happy moments? At 2.55pm on Sunday 25 January 1981 (the sixth day of Ronald Reagan's presidency), a VC-137C transport, nicknamed 'Freedom One' for the occasion, landed at Stewart Airport near the US Military Academy in West Point, NY, completing the final leg of a long journey that returned 52 freed American hostages to home soil for the first time since their imprisonment when Iranian terrorists took over the US Embassy in Tehran on 4 November 1979. Their ordeal in captivity had lasted 444 days. Hostage Michael Metrinko later told me that the Boeing VC-137C flight home was one the most joyous moments of his life. Flying home, Mike said, is what aviation is about.

Ronald Reagan is said to be an easy-going passenger during the special air mission flights, Caspar Weinberger a demanding one. The wife of a certain Washington dignitary is rumoured to insist on a certain colour of curtains when she flies one of the big Boeings. Just as it does in the airlines, a controversy over cigarette smoking (not Haig's, but everybody's) persists in the VIP airlift community. Equally, in an era of increasing terrorism, it is widely reported that the 89th MAW's C-135B and C-137C transports have countermeasures to foil heat-seeking missiles, such as ECM gear, chaff or flare decoys.

A final note about these changing times. It must be said that because the times have become more violent, the VIP transport mission includes the sad job of bringing home the casualties of the twilight war. The sight of a casket draped in the American flag, being offloaded from a C-135, has become more commonplace than any of us could ever have guessed. One of my saddest duties as an American diplomat was to appear at Andrews AFB, Maryland, in a snowstorm on 18 February 1979 to greet VC-135B 62-4127 of the 89th MAW when it returned from Kabul with the body of my friend Ambassador Adolph (Spike) Dubs. Up until that year, only one American ambassador had *ever* been assassinated, a statistic which seems beyond belief in today's world. Eight years after my own flight in a VC-135B, 10 months before the Soviet invasion of that tortured country, Dubs had been killed in a terrorist incident in Afghanistan.

4 Reconnaissance

When aircraft were first used to gather information, they were called scouts, a term pre-dating World War 1. The military reconnaissance mission began with reliance on a device known as the 'Mark One Eyeball' and by World War 2 graduated to the use of a remarkable variety of cameras. More recently, the reconnaissance mission has required a mind-boggling array of electronic gadgetry. The job remains, as it was in canvas-covered scout planes, to become well informed about a potential enemy. As one Washington wag put it, 'When we do it, it's called intelligence. When the other guy does it, it's called spying'.

Certain facts about the United States strategic reconnaissance mission by RC-135 aircraft are fully unclassified and available to anyone wishing to consult public documents. These include the serial numbers of RC-135 airframes; their power-plants, their units, and some aspects of their individual histories. Other facts will be missing from these pages, first because the author does not know them and, second, because he does not want to know. The 1 July 1985 report on US Air Force C-135 aircraft in inventory will be quoted again, but the part of this reported which describes the mission to be carried out says, simply, 'Operations are classified'.

In the book *Aerial Espionage*, Dick van der Aart says the obvious: 'America has always openly admitted the existence of the RC-135 electronic reconnaissance aircraft but has never released any details about its operational missions.' Many Americans heard of the RC-135 for the first time when press reports confirmed that a reconnaissance Boeing had been aloft at the same time as the 747 jetliner shot down by Soviet fighters on 1 September 1983 — although every attempt to establish some link between a reconnaissance flight over international waters and the Soviet decision to down an innocent airliner has failed totally.

Reconnaissance was almost certainly not one of the functions envisioned when the basic KC-135 airframe was designed in the 1950s. It soon became apparent, however, that the aircraft was an ideal platform for a variety of missions. Its size, speed and relatively long range made it a practical machine to carry electronic surveillance equipment on flights of extended duration along the borders of nations like the Soviet Union which do not encourage more open examination of their societies.

Below:
High over the Baltic Sea, this RC-135V reconnaissance aircraft, 64-14843, was intercepted and photographed by J35F Draken fighters of the Swedish Air Force. It can be assumed that Soviet fighters similarly escort RC-135V and other recce aircraft on their flights over international waters. *Swedish Air Force*

The strategic reconnaissance mission had previously been carried out mainly by converted bombers, such as the RB-47 Stratojet, and on occasion there were flash-points in the Cold War. On 1 July 1960 a RB-47H of the 55th Strategic Reconnaissance Wing, home-based at Offutt AFB, Nebraska, was shot down by a Soviet fighter over the Barents Sea. Where the reconnaissance role *was* being performed by a converted transport, there were hot moments, too, as on 15 April 1969 when an EC-121K Warning Star was shot down by North Korean fighters over the Sea of Japan. No such violence seems to have befallen a RC-135, and indeed there exists no reason why routine reconnaissance flights need be considered a provocation by anyone. Far from involving cloak and dagger antics, the typical RC-135 reconnaissance mission seems to involve long hours of boredom while flying at safe distances from danger, over international waters.

The strategic reconnaissance fleet (not including the weather reconnaissance force, a part of MAC) is managed by SAC on a worldwide basis. At least

a dozen variants of the RC-135 have been used for various missions. The location of crew stations is similar between the RC-135 missions but the specialised intelligence-gathering equipment varies widely. All SAC RC-135s have the airborne refuelling system which enables them to be refuelled in flight by tankers.

Bumps and Bulges

Internal and external appearance of the various RC-135 and WC-135 aircraft differs considerably and often only the most astute student of bumps and bulges can tell one model from another. As Boeing historian Alwyn T. Lloyd has pointed out, a plethora of antennas and bulges adorn the RC-135s, the varying configurations resulting from HF, VHF and UHF wire, probe, blade and bi-electric panel antenna found at various points on the aircraft, plus distinctive SLAR (side-ways looking airborne radar) cheeks installed on many airframes. Most of SAC's RC-135s belong to the 55th SRW located at the same place as SAC headquarters, Offutt AFB, Nebraska, others being assigned to the 6th SRW at Eilson AFB, Alaska. All of MAC's weather-reconnaissance WC-135s are assigned to the 55th Weather Reconnaissance Squadron at McClellan AFB, California.

The first C-135 reconnaissance aircraft was 55-3121, a conversion of the number four KC-135A initially employed for a wide-ranging series of tests aimed at deciding upon a definitive recce configuration. This aircraft joined the 55th SRW under Col William E. Riggs around the time

Below:
The four RC-135As were the last C-135s delivered and were used by the 1370th Photo Mapping Wing at Turner AFB, Georgia, for cartographic and geodetic survey missions. In 1972 all four RC-135A airframes transferred from MAC to SAC, and by 1979 they had reverted to tanking duties under the designation KC-135D. *Boeing*

the wing took up residence at Offutt on 16 August 1966. The aircraft carried only three or four electronics operators, known as Crows, and trailed a capsule packed with listening gear on a 12,000ft (3,658m) wire. This listening-post arrangement was only the first of several configurations in which this aircraft was employed. At one time it had a row of five fence aerials along its spine, causing British spotters to give it the nickname 'Porcupine'. As will be noted elsewhere, 55-3121 became a KC-135R and later a trainer under the designation RC-135T before being lost on 26 February 1985 at Valdez, Alaska.

The success of this first recce aircraft led to a second machine, 59-1465, joining the SAC reconnaissance fleet. The two were designated KC-135R (a term later used for a re-engined tanker) and were employed on a worldwide basis in the strategic collection role until 59-1465 was lost on 17 July 1967.

Enter the RC-135D

Although three more KC-135Rs were operated by the 55th SRW, the first model to have its reconnaissance role correctly appended as a prefix was the RC-135D. Following tests with several airframes, among them NKC-135A 55-3132, the RC-135D was introduced featuring the elongated 'Hog Nose' (also often called a thimble nose) and a cylindrical SLAR fairing forward of the wing root. These aircraft retained the original water-burning J57 engines and were assigned to the 6th SRW at Eilson AFB, Alaska, where the lack of range resulting from not having turbofans was not

Top:
Seen in mid to late 1965, aircraft 55-3121 was the first reconnaissance-configured C-135. Originally a JKC-135A, it moved to SAC in 1963 for CIA projects 'Briar Patch' and 'Iron Lung' and was redesignated KC-135R. Later, this aircraft was used as a trainer with the designation RC-135T, until its loss at Valdez, Alaska, on 26 February 1985. *Paul Bennett*

Above:
Taking off from Mildenhall with relatively smoke-free turbofan engines in June 1983 is aircraft 62-4135 of SAC's 55th Strategic Reconnaissance Wing. This aircraft served as a RC-135M before being converted to RC-135W standards. *Paul Bennett*

critical. As will be seen, however, the RC-135D turned up occasionally in South-East Asia as well.

Four aircraft were used in the RC-135D configuration. They were followed by what may have been the most striking of SAC's reconnaissance aircraft, this being the one-of-a-kind RC-135E. A conversion of the turbofan-powered C-135B transport, the RC-135E has in common with other recce variants introduced so far the fact of being past history. According to researcher David Donald, successful tests of a SLAR pod (apparently the same tests which preceded the RC-135D) led to the sole RC-135E, *Lisa Ann* (62-4137), which was readily identified by the two pods slung underneath the wing inboard of the engines plus an even more distinctive feature, a giant wrap-around glassfibre fairing for a Hughes-built SLAR located in the forward fuselage. In fact it has never been certain whether the glassfibre encircled all or merely a significant part of the forward fuselage. The unique RC-135E flew its missions with the 6th SRW at Eilson but was lost on 5 June 1969 over the Bering Sea, apparently

because of massive structural failure of the wrap-around radome.

A number of other airframes in the reconnaissance series are no longer flying in the configuration for that mission. The third and fourth KC-135R aeroplanes (58-0124, 58-0126) were modified in the 1960s and employed in the photographic reconnaissance role with camera ports cut into the cargo door, thimble nose housing an extended radome, and blade antennae on the dorsal spine of the fuselage. The 'Hog Nose' radome, incidentally, adds just under 3ft (1m) to the length of the several RC-135 models which have it; the radome is not hinged but is easily removed on a trolley for access to the radar. The final two KC-135R airframes were restored to the tanker role by 1980.

Into the Crucible

Combat operations in the long and costly slugfest and Hanoi will be discussed again in connection with the tanker mission in Chapter 9. The strategic reconnaissance mission in South-East Asia (not to

Above:
Toward the end of the South-East Asia war, RC-135U 64-14847 flew 'Combat Sent' missions over the Gulf of Tonkin, detecting signals in the fusing and guidance systems of North Vietnamese SAMs. The RC-135U is noted for 'rabbit ears' antennae, chin radar and enlarged SLAR cheeks. Years later, in 1981, the aircraft was in the UK. *John Dunnell*

be confused with the tactical recce job carried out by RF-101C Voodoos and RF-4C Phantoms) is a vital ingredient of the C-135 story and belongs here. This mission was originally the purview of the Boeing RB-47 Stratojet which handled offshore, oblique photography and its EB-47 Stratojet variant which collected electronic intelligence under a programme called 'Box Top'. As early as 1963, SAC had decided to phase out the Stratojet and soon decided that a similar mission could be flown by a modified C-135B transport, which acquired the designation RC-135M.

RC-135M was another designation which is now past history and therefore does not appear in the Tinker Report quoted throughout this narrative. Six airframes acquired this appellation. Features of

the RC-135M included the thimble nose and teardrop fairings on the rear fuselage. Flying with the 4252nd Strategic Reconnaissance Wing out of Yokota AB, Japan, the RC-135M reportedly was first employed on reconnaissance directed towards mainland China and the western Soviet Union.

By 1966 the RC-135M had replaced the Stratojet as the principal long-range reconnaissance collector in the Vietnam combat zone. In fact the last RB-47 was phased out of the theatre by 10 January 1967. The RC-135M carried a crew of up to 14 electronic specialists, the hard-working Crows, jammed into confined quarters and surrounded by a science-fiction maze of equipment. Two of the missions it flew were given the names 'Cotton Candy' and 'Iron Lung'. It can be assumed that the RC-135M was gathering signals intelligence (SIGINT) by monitoring Hanoi's radar and radio transmissions.

On 25 August 1967 the 82nd Strategic Reconnaissance Squadron was organised and shortly thereafter moved to Kadena to handle RC-135M reconnaissance missions. The huge

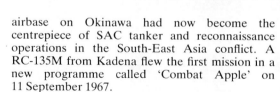

airbase on Okinawa had now become the centrepiece of SAC tanker and reconnaissance operations in the South-East Asia conflict. A RC-135M from Kadena flew the first mission in a new programme called 'Combat Apple' on 11 September 1967.

'Combat Apple' involved flying 12-hour orbits over the Gulf of Tonkin, and later over Laos too, collecting electronic intelligence with special attention to picking up indications of signals from the 'Fan Song' radar associated with Hanoi's SA-2 'Guideline' surface-to-air missiles. These signals enabled US experts to pinpoint the location of SAM sites. Areas of intense search for them included North Vietnam, Hainan Island and the Demilitarised Zone. At first there were about 50 or 60 'Combat Apple' missions a month, but they soon levelled off to about 30. The 'Combat Apple' aircraft regularly flew other SAC reconnaissance missions as well. This had replaced an earlier mission which was also the collection of electronic

Above:
The weather reconnaissance mission is carried out by the 55th Weather Reconnaissance Squadron at McClellan AFB, California. Originally built as a C-135B Stratolifter and converted to WC-135B standard in 1965, aircraft 61-2667 is seen at McClellan on 28 October 1967 but was still in service in the same capacity two decades later.
Steve Kraus

intelligence. In this case, it involved peripheral reconnaissance over the Yellow Sea, East China Sea and Gulf of Tonkin with the objective of collecting electronic intelligence on the communist nations' order of battle.

When the RC-135M went 'up North', the MiGs came out. For a time Hanoi's air defence authorities toyed with the idea of intercepting a RC-135M. Published accounts tell of F-4 Phantoms accompanying the 'Combat Apple' aircraft on its trip to the edge of enemy terrain, the Phantoms remaining so close that their own radar images blurred with that of the RC-135M. Unaware that the RC-135M was escorted by 'little friends', the MiGs came after what they thought was a big slow Boeing only to find accompanying F-4s looking down their throats. After this happened a few times, an unspoken truce took effect: the RC-135M remained a certain distance away from North Vietnamese airspace and the MiGs left it alone.

The RC-135M was not without its problems. Regardless of all measures taken to prevent it, South-East Asia's torrential rains found their way into the turbofan thrust reversers. The water seeped into and shorted the control circuits and caused the TF33 engines to go into reverse! This often happened just after take-off, while climbing in Vietnam's tropical thunderstorms, causing the Stratotanker to yaw violently.

Recce 'up North'

During the 'Linebacker' campaigns of 1972, the RC-135M began flying an overland route on the 'Combat Apple' missions. With the aircraft prowling in the same area as the heavily-defended Ho Chi Minh Trail and other infiltration routes, the relative safety of the recce crews became a thing of the past and the risk from missiles, MiGs and Triple-A became more serious than ever. The MiGs tried again. North Vietnam had threatened to shoot down a B-52, so far without success, and a RC-135M would be a coveted consolation prize. MiGs again made several attempts to intercept the RC-135M, again being suckered by Phantoms which snuggled beneath the Stratotanker to blend with its radar image. In addition to being stalked by the enemy, RC-135M crews suffered from overscheduling: one 'Combat Apple' aircraft flew 12-hour missions over the Gulf of Tonkin while another circled over Laos, doubling demand on the Stratotanker and posing a severe strain when, most of the time, only two airframes were readily available.

As noted earlier, SAC had introduced the less powerful and shorter-range RC-135D variant to reconnaissance missions elsewhere, primarily those operated along the Soviet periphery from Eilson AFB, Alaska. On rare instances when an RC-135D was substituted for the 'Combat Apple' mission in South-East Asia in lieu of the usual RC-135M, aircrews reported some odd frustrations. Accustomed to the dry Arctic cold, the RC-135D leaked heavily in South-East Asia's hot humidity; the less powerful J57 engines were an aggravation to mechanics spoiled by the TF33.

In the main though, it was the RC-135M variant which flew the 'Combat Apple' and other missions for the duration of the South-East Asia war, a period of nearly six years. By the time they ceased

Above:
Returning from a reconnaissance mission, RC-135U Stratotanker 64-14847 is settling down to land at RAF Mildenhall, England, in 1980. *John Dunnell*

operations the aircraft had flown over 3,250 operational sorties for 39,286 orbit hours. They had provided MiG warning, assistance to search and rescue (SAR) operations, and had collected signals intelligence, a term which includes electronic intelligence.

Later, this narrative will introduce the RC-135U aircraft, which remains in service today and which was the final variant of the Stratotanker to fly recce missions in the South-East Asia conflict. The RC-135U flew under a programme called 'Combat Sent', and was said to be the most capable and elaborate special-mission variant ever. There were only two RC-135Us to cover the entire world, so one spent about three months each year at Kadena and devoted some of this stay to operations against North Vietnam. 'Combat Sent' detected not merely the location of SAM sites, but changes in the fusing and guidance signals of North Vietnamese SAMs. The RC-135U had a problem remaining in position during orbit near the enemy's terrain, however. Weight and drag of the RC-135U in its original configuration was much greater than that of the RC-135D/M, yet the aircraft was tasked to fly at higher altitude. The RC-135U had no difficulty maintaining this height with a portion of its fuel capacity expended, but after taking on fuel from a KC-135A brother, it was too heavy. On two occasions the RC-135U stalled and fell like a rock until a startled crew could regain control. This happened so suddenly and so dramatically that crew members were thrown around inside the fuselage and terrified almost witless. Eventually the problem was solved with minor adjustments in fuel load and configuration, but the RC-135U retained the nickname 'lead sled' because of its reputation for being exceedingly heavy.

Another part of the reconnaissance story in South-East Asia concerns the missions flown by the Lockheed SR-71 Blackbird. These were also supported from Kadena, with refuelling provided by the KC-135Q tanker. The KC-135Q force grew to 10 aircraft by 30 October 1967 and remained an important part of the war effort thereafter. The KC-135Q tanker will be discussed further in Chapter 9.

Weather Recce
The weather reconnaissance job, in peace and war, is the purview of Military Airlift Command which operates the WC-135B aircraft. This again is a function which the Stratotanker took over from the older Stratojet (in this case the WB-47) as well as the propeller-driven WB-50 Superfortress.

The weather recce people are best known as 'hurricane hunters' for their role in flying directly into the tropical depressions so familiar to people living near the South China Sea or the Florida coast. In fact detecting and analysing hurricanes is but one small aspect of the worldwide job of evaluating weather and relating it to military plans of all kinds.

To return again to the Tinker Report which gives us a listing of Stratotanker variants in inventory on 1 July 1985, the MAC weather reconnaissance model is the first to be mentioned.

● **WC-135B** is the designation assigned to the only Military Airlift Command weather reconnaissance craft still in service. When last counted for our report, the number of WC-135Bs totalled seven:

Serial No	Engine	Used by
61-2665/2666	TF33-P-5	55th WRS/McClellan AFB, California
61-2667	TF33-P-5	55th WRS/McClellan AFB, California
61-2670	TF33-P-5	55th WRS/McClellan AFB, California
61-2672/2674	TF33-P-5	55th WRS/McClellan AFB, California

A blue-white band reading 'WEATHER' is the distinctive marking which sets this aircraft apart from other Stratotankers.

Originally, 10 C-135Bs were converted to weather recce configuration. Three of these were subsequently converted to C-135C standard.

Special equipment installed in these aircraft includes the AN/ALQ-25 meteorological system and a separate equipment array known as the Atmospheric Research Equipment (ARE) suite. They are also equipped to receive in-flight refuelling. The WC-135B aircraft are an integral part of the Air Force weather surveillance service, and although nominally assigned to one base, they actually operate around the world.

● **RC-135S**, to continue the round-up of variants assigned to the reconnaissance mission as of 1 July 1985, is the appellation for three Stratotanker rebuilds, all fitted or retrofitted with TF33 engines, with large external dipole aerials around the forward fuselage, blisters around the rear fuselage, and various windows and projecting dustbins and pods. One of the trio, aircraft 61-2664 was lost on 16 March 1981, leaving in service the remaining two:

Serial No	Engine	Used by
61-2662	TF33-P-5	6th SRW/Eilson AFB, Alaska
61-2663	TF33-P-5	6th SRW/Eilson AFB, Alaska

These aircraft, too, are equipped for air-to-air refuelling. The Air Force report covers their mission by saying that they are 'used to gather information on potential adversaries on a world-wide basis. [They perform] specialised intelligence gathering.' One of several variants with the ubiquitous 'Hog Nose', the RC-135S seems to be the Stratotanker mentioned in connection with the Korean Air Lines incident.

Associated with programmes bearing the names 'Rivet Ball' and 'Cobra Ball', the RC-135S is usually seen in the Pacific. The aircraft always have the thimble nose, but the external appearance of different airframes varies considerably, with differing numbers of large circular windows and of 'towel rack' antennae on the forward fuselage. It has been reported that the RC-135S performs both telemetry and photography of Soviet missile re-entry vehicles, the picture-taking being the reason for the circular windows, with the upper surface of the wings painted black to prevent glare from distorting the pictures.

The RC-135S aircraft have also been seen with a variety of teardrop fairings on the rear fuselage and blister fairings farther forward. Numerous blade aerials appear above and below the fuselage.

Aircraft 59-1491 (built as a KC-135A, converted to RC-135D and again converted to RC-135S) was the only aircraft of this variant to be powered by J57 engines. It was lost in a crash at Eilson AFB, Alaska, on 10 March 1969. The more recent examples in the RC-135S series have been powered by TF33 turbofans.

● **RC-135U** is the designation for another SAC reconnaissance aircraft, already introduced as the 'heavy' in Vietnam, which was grotesquely modified for the advanced electronics intelligence role with gigantic SLAR installations on the side of the forward fuselage, and various arrays of antennas, probes and blisters at the tip of the tail and the top of the fin. Three airframes were modified to RC-135U standard in 1971, one of them (64-14848) subsequently being revised to RC-135V status, leaving just two machines:

Serial No	Engine	Used by
64-14847	TF33-P-9	55th SRW/Offutt AFB, Nebraska
64-14849	TF33-P-9	55th SRW/Offutt AFB, Nebraska

Again, few details of the actual reconnaissance mission performed by these aircraft have been made public. The aircraft are equipped to receive in-flight refuelling.

● **RC-135V** is next in the family of SAC reconnaissance machines, this designation applying to seven rebuilds of RC-135Cs plus one RC-135U with SLAR cheeks, long thimble nose, ventral arrays of blade aerials and a probe on the right wingtip. All eight remain in service:

Serial No	Engine	Used by
63-9792	TF33-P-9	55th SRW/Offutt AFB, Nebraska
64-14841/14846	TF33-P-9	55th SRW/Offutt AFB, Nebraska
64-14848	TF33-P-9	55th SRW/Offutt AFB, Nebraska

● **RC-135W** seems to be the most recent designation for yet another family of SAC reconnaissance aircraft, these being generally similar to the RC-135V with thimble nose radomes, SLAR cheeks, probes, wires and masts. There are six in inventory:

Serial No	Engine	Used by
62-4131/4132	TF33-P-5	55th SRW/Offutt AFB, Nebraska
62-4134/4135	TF33-P-5	55th SRW/Offutt AFB, Nebraska
62-4138/4139	TF33-P-5	55th SRW/Offutt AFB, Nebraska

Left:
The RC-135V is the most numerous of Stratotanker reconnaissance variants, numbering some eight examples. Silhouetted between the mainwheels are massive blade aerials on the lower fuselage. Aircraft 64-14844 was seen at RAF Fairford, England, in 1983.
John Dunnell

Below left:
RC-135W 62-4139 of the 55th SRW based at Offutt AFB, Nebraska, on approach to RAF Mildenhall, England, in May 1985. This airframe began life as a C-135B transport for the Military Air Transport Service (MATS), being delivered in September 1962, and was later a RC-135M before being upgraded to RC-135W standard. Note the electronics package on the fuselage side and the inverted T-shaped antennae under the fuselage. *John Dunnell*

Some of these machines, after being built as C-135B transports, spent a brief period in RC-135M configuration before becoming RC-135W aircraft. They are equipped to receive in-flight refuelling.

● **TC-135S** is a final designation which seems to belong in a chapter about the reconnaissance role. One such aircraft was in the 1 July 1985 report:

Serial No	Engine	Used by
62-4133	TF33-P-5	6th SRW/Eilson AFB, Alaska

This aircraft too was originally produced as a C-135B and assigned to the Military Air Transport Service for airlift operations. It was next assigned to Air Force Systems command to provide communications support in space programmes. It was modified to an Advanced Range Instrumented Aircraft (ARIA) in 1979 and was operated as an EC-135B until May 1984 when converted to TC-135S as a flight trainer for the RC-135S 'and the forthcoming RC-135X', the latter being a designation about which almost no information is available.

KAL Shootdown
So what about the connection between the RC-135 reconnaissance aircraft and the Soviet shootdown of a Korean Air Lines Boeing 747 jetliner? Was the shootdown on 1 September 1983, which resulted in the deaths of 269 people, somehow connected with American reconnaissance operations? Was the airliner itself somehow involved in collecting intelligence with the RC-135 in the air as some sort of back-up? As ridiculous as these assertions sound, they were made at the time by people who wanted to be regarded as serious. Perhaps the best acquittal of the US reconnaissance effort in the KAL incident comes not from a supporter of the Reagan administration but from one of its staunchest critics. Pulitzer Prize-winning journalist Seymour M. Hersh spent three years researching the KAL shootdown only to conclude, in the end, what should have been obvious all along: the Soviets shot down an innocent airliner which was lost and violated their airspace by accident.

Moscow, which had given Hersh access to Soviet leaders, must have been disappointed when he was unable to find a conspiracy. At the time of the incident a high-ranking Soviet official, Chief of Staff Nikolai Ogarkov, loomed above a press conference audience and pointed on a map at the track of an RC-135 operating over the Sea of Okhotsk. Ogarkov said that the RC-135 had

gotten confused with the airliner and that, in the dark, Soviet Sukhoi Su-21 ('Flagon-F') fighters shot down the wrong aircraft. It may not be an accident that Ogarkov was not in office for long thereafter.

According to Hersh, the RC-135 was aloft that day on a mission code-named 'Cobra Ball' for the Air Force's Electronic Security Command. The very first of SAC's many RC-135 aircraft was 55-3121, the converted number four KC-135A which came to the 55th Strategic Reconnaissance Wing in the 1960s, just when the wing moved from Forbes AFB, Kansas, to Offutt AFB, Nebraska. From then until now, with the RC-135W flying today and the RC-135X cryptically mentioned in the Air Force report, so far as anyone can determine, *no RC-135 has ever been involved in a shooting incident*. So why was a RC-135 in the air on the day the KAL airliner was shot down? The answer is stunningly simple, so simple that neither Ogarkov nor Hersh are needed to provide it. *RC-135s are in the air every day*. There is no more to the involvement of the reconnaissance aircraft in the KAL shootdown than that.

A Glimpse Inside
The internal layout of the various RC-135 models will have to remain largely a mystery since very few details have been disclosed. Each individual aircraft (not merely each variant) is thought to have a different crew operating cabin with consoles of equipment used to intercept signals or take photographs.

The function of signals intelligence (SIGINT) is to locate and analyse hostile signals and to glean intelligence data from them. It can be supposed that the job of analysing what is found during a mission actually begins before the aircraft has landed; thus some of the crew members aboard may be analysts as well as Crows. The role of women in the US armed forces is evident once again, for the analyst and Crow functions can be filled by females.

One of the few released views of the inside of a RC-135, unfortunately too poor for reproduction, shows a single operator's station with an oscilloscope used to display radar wave patterns, perhaps to break up their pulse for deeper analysis. The scope is, in turn, surrounded by an array of equipment and gauges which looks like the interior of some fictitious space ship.

For now, little more can be said of the reconnaissance operations conducted by the members of the C-135 family. It can only be hoped that people like SAC's historian are keeping files so that the full story may be told one day. Suffice to say, for now, that the recce mission is of utmost importance and the RC-135 seems to be performing it very ably indeed.

5 AWACS

The Boeing E-3 Sentry, developed as the AWACS (Airborne Warning & Control System) for the US Air Force, NATO and Saudi Arabia, is technically *not* part of the KC-135 series at all, and would not have been included in this narrative but for its external resemblance. This flying surveillance centre was, of course, conceived from the Boeing 707 airliner design. As originally planned in 1970, the AWACS aircraft would have been the most expensive flying machine ever built at a price of $107 million per copy and would have been powered by eight TF34 turbofan engines, two each on the engine pylons already associated with the design. As a cost-cutting measure, the E-3A Sentry was built instead with four TF33-100-100A engines. Even so, its cost doubled and it remains, today, the most costly individual flying machine ever built.

The US Air Force pioneered the use of overland surveillance platforms starting with the Lockheed EC-121 Warning Star, built in several variants and based upon the Super Constellation. In the South-East Asia conflict, EC-121s using the callsign 'Disco' were teamed with offshore surveillance vessels, called 'Red Crown', to provide American fighter pilots with warning and advice when MiGs were scrambled against them. The EC-121 remained very much in service until as late as 1980 (the loss of one aircraft off the North Korean coast has already been mentioned), but a jet-powered replacement for the EC-121 was clearly needed.

As early as the 1960s, radar technology had come to the point where, with greater power and rapid digital processing, an over-the-horizon (OTH) capability could be achieved. In addition, new radars capable of detecting the doppler shift in received frequency caused by relative motion between the target and the radar platform were able to detect and track high-speed aircraft flying close to the ground, without becoming confused by ground clutter. A new flying radar station would be able to employ the new radars and other sensors to detect hostile aircraft under circumstances previously considererd impossible.

An operational requirement for the new radar aircraft, or AWACS, was issued to the airframe industry, and both Boeing and McDonnell Douglas received funding in 1967 to study installing the new radars and sensors in an existing aircraft, such as the Boeing 707 or Douglas DC-8. Douglas's proposal initially called for a military

Below:
The Boeing family of airborne early warning and control aircraft is based upon the Boeing 707 airliner rather than the KC-135 tanker. First in the series was this EC-137D, 71-1407, which served as prototype for the E-3A and eventually acquired the latter designation. *Boeing*

Above:
Production E-3A Sentry 83-1674 lifts off from its Boeing plant with closely-related 707 in the background. All E-3A aircraft are operated by the 552nd Airborne Warning & Control Wing headquartered at Tinker AFB, Oklahoma. *USAF*

Below:
Boeing E-3A Sentry 76-1607 on final approach. AWACs pilots go through a different training syllabus to those who fly the KC-135, since their aircraft is a very different derivative of the Boeing 707 rather than a modification of the Stratotanker. *John Dunnell*

Bottom:
Aircraft 79-0443, or LX-N90443, was the third E-3A Sentry AWACS delivered to NATO forces. These aircraft wear the NATO emblem but no national markings.
Paul Bennett

version of the 'stretched' DC-8 Series 63 but its final design was based upon the shorter DC-8 Series 62. Boeing engineers initially examined an odd-looking version of the Model 707-320 airliner with the now-familiar rotodome, housing the radar equipment, mounted on a swept-forward tail fin. Later the rotodome acquired its own housing on the dorsal spine of the aircraft.

On 8 July 1970 Boeing was awarded the prime contract for the AWACS aircraft. At this time the company's proposed design still made use of eight TF34 turbofan engines. The antenna for the main radar, back-to-back with IFF (identification, friend or foe) and communications antenna, was mounted on two 11ft (3.35m) struts above the rear fuselage and streamlined by adding two D-shaped radomes of glass fibre sandwich which turned the girder-like antenna array into a deep circular rotodome some 30ft (9.14m) in diameter and 6ft (1.83m) deep. The rotating mass weighed 3,395lb (1,540kg) and the rotodome itself was angled 2.5° downwards to minimise aerodynamic movements on the turntable. The rotodome turned very slowly to keep the bearings lubricated; when on station it rotated at six revolutions per minute and its beam was electronically scanned under computer control.

Enter the EC-137D

The initial contract to Boeing was for the conversion of two Model 707-320B airliners, designated EC-137D by the Air Force and assigned serials 71-1407/1408. These aircraft were to conduct flight trials with competing radars offered by Hughes and Westinghouse. The first EC-137D flew at Seattle on 9 February 1972, by which time the decision had been made to power the aircraft with four TF33s. In fact the EC-137D prototype was outwardly identical to the E-3A Sentry AWACS aircraft to follow. After a 93-minute maiden flight, project pilot Jim Gannett proclaimed that all initial test objectives had been met. There had been some concern that the big rotodome would encounter aerodynamic drag problems but, in the end, it worked as advertised.

Between 4 April and 5 September 1972 the two EC-137D airframes were wrung out in the Seattle area, each making 49 test flights, for the purpose of evaluating the competing radars by Hughes and Westinghouse. At stake was a huge purchase order. Flying against target aircraft such as F-4 Phantoms and B-52 Stratofortresses provided by the US Air Force, EC-137D crews evaluated the two radars for their performance in varying conditions, with varying land and sea backgrounds, at differing temperatures, heights and angles. In October 1972 the Air Force announced that the Westinghouse AN/APY-1 radar had been selected for the production E-3A Sentry.

Into Production

Production of an initial batch of 24 E-3A Sentry aircraft was authorised in April 1975 with deliveries to the 552nd Airborne Warning & Control Wing at Tinker AFB, Oklahoma, over the period March 1977 to March 1981. First flight of the windowless, rotodome-equipped E-3A took place on 31 October 1975. Serials for the initial batch were 73-1674/1675 (two), 75-0556/0561 (six), 76-1604/1607 (four), 77-0351/0356 (six), 78-0576/0578 (three) and 79-0001/0003 (three). The wing received its first E-3A on 24 March 1977 and attained initial operating capability (IOC) with the aircraft a year later.

With further production authorised in the late 1970s, from the 22nd airframe onwards an overwater capability was incorporated and, from airframe number 24, the E-3A was made capable of being linked to the Joint Tactical Information Distribution System (JTIDS), shared by all NATO forces.

US Air Force aircraft Nos 25-34 are designated Standard E-3As but these have been upgraded since 1984 to E-3C standard with five additional crew display consoles, five more UHF radio installations and the 'Have Quick' anti-jamming improvements. Meanwhile, the 24 original core E-3As have been progressively upgraded to E-3B standard. These have the CC-2 computer (faster and with roughly quadrupled storage capacity as compared with the original), extra consoles and UHF radios, ECM-resistant voice communications and radio teleprinter.

On a normal patrol the AWACS aircraft cruises at Mach 0.72 at an altitude of 29,000ft (8,800m). Under these conditions the radar has a range of over 230 miles (368km) against low-level targets. The AWACS can remain on patrol for nine to 11 hours and this can be extended to 22 hours by in-flight refuelling. American and Saudi AWACS aircraft are supported by tankers but those operated by NATO are not.

The US Air Force's population of 34 airframes will eventually all be brought up to the E-3C standard. They operate all over the world with the 552nd Wing, which in turn operates six squadrons, the 960th AW&CS detached at NS Keflavik, Iceland, the 961st AW&CS detached at Kadena AB, Okinawa, and the 963rd to 966th AW&CS at the Tinker home-base, the number 962 having been skipped. To support these aircraft, permanent overseas detachment are kept in Iceland and at Kadena. The AWACS aircraft operate in partnership with EC-135 and WC-135 support aircraft of the 8th Tactical Deployment Control Squadron, and with various tanker forces.

NATO Airborne Warning

At various milestones in its career, AWACS could

have been shot down by a penny-pinching Office of Management & Budget (OMB), or by Congress. At first the high cost per airframe was an issue when the type was being built solely for the US forces. The figure of $107 million went over $200 million, when not adjusted for the inflation of the late 1970s, making the E-3A more expensive even than a B-1B bomber.

The next milestone was purchase by Saudi Arabia, a step which was opposed by some Congressmen and viewed by critics as a threat to Israel. Coming on the heels of an exceedingly controversial sale of F-15A Eagle fighters to that country, the sale nearly foundered. Still later, AWACS survived opponents of the plan to supply the aircraft to NATO, to be operated by multi-national crews with US assistance. No other aircraft type in NATO service is operated by such crews, or lacks the individual national insignia of a using country, as does the E-3A. The first batch of 10 E-3A aircraft for NATO (79-0442/0451) was ordered in the late 1970s. Orders for a further eight (79-0452/0459) came next.

It had been apparent that the operation of national AWACS fleets was too unwieldy and too expensive for most of the NATO allies and that a multi-national force made good sense from a variety of perspectives. The NATO aircraft was first delivered on 22 January 1982, the NATO fleet being civil-registered in Luxembourg and based at Geilenkirchen, West Germany.

These 18 aircraft were flown to Dornier's factory at Oberpfaffenhofen, where they were completed to the NATO standard. Among their special features are a third HF radio teletype for overwater use, as well as a radio-teletype for hard-copy communication with maritime forces. They also have a new data analysis and programming group, and hard-points under the inner wings where pylons could be added if needed. Like their US Air Force counterparts, the NATO E-3A aircraft normally fly extremely accurate racetrack patterns in the sky while on station. Because of their multi-national crews, it is sometimes said that even the most trivial decision on the NATO-AWACS base at Geilenkirchen must be reached after careful deliberation by the representatives of all 15 countries! The Luxembourg registrations correspond to the serial numbers (LX-N90445 for 79-0445) and the aircraft bear the arms of the Grand Duchy on their tails!

The Royal Saudi Air Force's AWACS fleet of KE-3A Sentrys, powered by four GE/SNECMA CFM56 turbofans (military designation F108-CF-100), the same powerplant found on newly re-engined KC-135Rs, is said to have been slightly downgraded by the removal of some sensitive equipment found on the American version and by deletion of JTIDS.

Still, the KE-3A for Saudi Arabia is a going concern and officials in Riyadh claim that the programmed fleet of five AWACS aircraft can provide better early-warning capability than would be possible with a network of 48 ground-based radars. The five aircraft in Saudi service were to be based first at Dhahran, later moving to Kharji.

Western aircraft spotters had their first glimpse of the Saudi early warning craft on 1 July 1986 when a Sentry for the Royal Saudi Air Force was delivered from the Boeing facility at Renton via RAF Mildenhall, England, carrying Saudi serial 1801 on the fin but full USAF titles and national insignia. The aircraft continued onwards on 2 July to Riyadh to become the first Boeing assigned to the newly activated No 18 Squadron. The aircraft was notable for the fat engine nacelles associated with the CFM56 powerplant.

It is understood that five airframes are intended for the AWACS early-warning function and that a further eight will have AWACS capability but will be employed primarily as tankers, the first Boeing aircraft to combine the two functions. All 13 aircraft are to be powered by the CFM56 engine. It appeared that US Air Force serials 82-0066/0076 and 83-0510/0511 had been assigned to the 13 Saudi airframes.

As usual, whenever an AWACS aircraft flies anywhere, controversy goes hand-in-hand with the Saudi sale. Proponents of it argue that the aircraft will contribute to regional security and provide an additional deterrent against Russian adventurism in the region where much of the world's oil is located. The Sentry is easy to sell on this basis, for it provides a significant military capability whilst remaining unarmed! Supporters of Israel insist, however, that the Sentry — together with F-15 Eagles sold to Saudi Arabia — is a threat to the small Jewish state. The sale of the KE-3A Sentry to Saudi Arabia dates back to the late 1970s and has its origins in the Carter administration, long delays being due in part to the difficulty of obtaining Congressional approval. While the sale to Saudi Arabia was still little more than an idea — an unpopular one in some quarters — Israel quietly acquired its own early-warning craft in the form of the Grumman E-2C Hawkeye.

A Pakistani AWACS?

If Boeing's flying surveillance platform evoked some controversy in the Middle East, in South Asia the situation was even worse. Once again, supporters of the E-3A Sentry were making that most persuasive of arguments — that the aircraft improves military capabilities yet is totally unarmed.

In 1986 the Reagan administration offered to sell Pakistan an early-warning aircraft with an electronic reach extending hundreds of miles into

The very first Stratotanker built, 55-3118 has served for many years as an airborne command post. Here it is depicted during a visit to Hickam AFB, Hawaii, in the late 1960s. *Nicholas M. Williams*

Indian territory, a move it said was justified by tensions in neighbouring Afghanistan. Gen Mohammed Zia ul-Haq's regime had rejected US proposals dating to 1980 for ground-based radar or balloon systems for installation on the Afghan border. Both Islamabad and Washington seemed to be exaggerating the Afghan air threat — which in reality had consisted only of incursions within six miles (9.6km) of the border — to justify sale of an AWACS which would almost certainly be used not against Afghanistan but against India.

A choice of the Grumman E-2C Hawkeye or the Boeing E-3A Sentry was understood to have been offered, although Zia unquestionably was lobbying for the latter. A possible factor in the arrangement was the peculiar fact that there had always been better relations between the air forces of the US and Pakistan than between the two countries' policymakers. It remained exceedingly difficult to understand how Pakistan — a nation widely suspected of clandestinely developing nuclear weapons — needed even the simpler Hawkeye, let alone the ultra-sophisticated Sentry. Worse, controversy over the AWACS offer erupted on the eve of a visit to India by Soviet leader Mikhail Gorbachev. At a time when India's Prime Minister Rajiv Gandhi (himself a former pilot of Boeing 707s) was under pressure to improve ties with the US and the West, the offer of AWACS to his traditional adversary might cause him to purchase additional MiG-29 fighters in a deal with Gorbachev instead.

It is thought that a US Air Force E-3A Sentry was taken to Pakistan for the specific purpose of being shown not merely to air staff officers but to Zia himself. The Sentry clearly is a prestige item, conferring a status which the Hawkeye does not, and the possible sale was likely to be debated vigorously.

Ironically, no one had foreseen so many export prospects for the E-3A Sentry. Yet at the very time the E-3A was being considered by still another nation, the export market was being cited by the competition as one of the reasons why the locally-built product should be chosen instead. If Britain would procure Nimrod instead of Sentry, the argument went, foreign sales of the former would assure British jobs.

A British AWACS?

Visitors to the 1986 Farnborough Air Show were treated to a display by Boeing of a large-scale model of the E-3A Sentry in Royal Air Force markings. A few believed that the sight of a 3ft (1m) Sentry model adorned in RAF roundels was something new. 'Oh, no', shrugged an insider, 'that's the same display model they used 10 years ago [in 1976] when they were first trying to sell the thing to us.'

Great Britain has now decided upon its early warning aircraft for the remainder of the century. Near the end of 1986 there had been increasing uncertainty over the future of the RAF's Nimrod AEW3 and the American-built AWACS — rejected by the RAF *at a lower price* during those first sales attempts a decade earlier — was chosen for Britain's forces. In further irony, the NATO version of the aircraft frequently calls at RAF Waddington, which now becomes a potential late customer for the E-3's capabilities. In fact, a NATO E-3A Sentry had made a special flight to Waddington to demonstrate the system to Britain's defence chief George Younger.

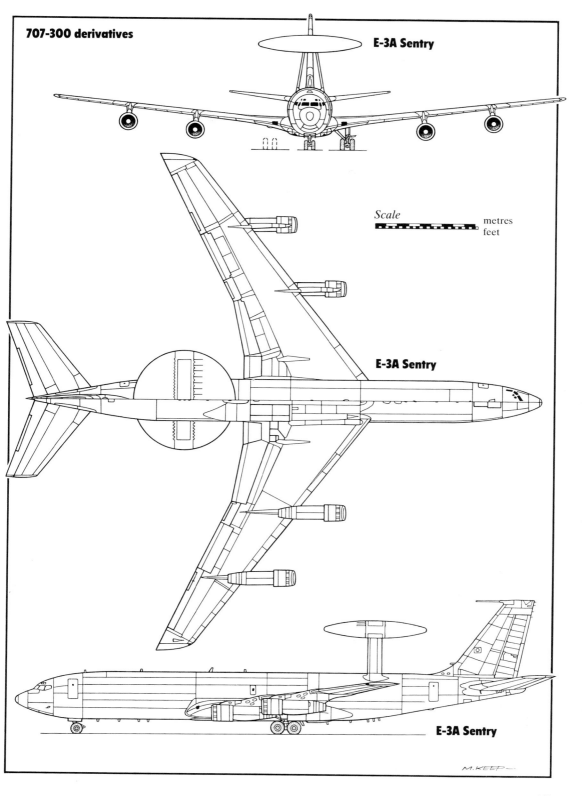

707-300 derivatives

E-3A Sentry

Scale

metres
feet

E-3A Sentry

E-3A Sentry

M. KEEP

Above:
Typical 'plain Jane' SAC KC-135A 57-2594 lifts off from Hickam AFB, Hawaii, on 1 February 1968. *Nicholas M. Williams*

Below:
The distinctive shape of the CFM56 engines is apparent in this view of re-engined KC-135R Stratotanker 60-0365 of the 28th Bomb Wing, seen on a visit to England on 6 December 1986. *Peter R. Foster*

Above:
The essence of the KC-135 Stratotanker and its refuelling mission is captured in this view of the row assembled for the KC-135 celebration at the International Air Tattoo, RAF Fairford, England, in 1985. The Ohio ANG aircraft in the foregound illustrates the use of the probe and drogue refuelling systems. *Anthony Thornborough*

Above:
RC-135V reconnaissance aircraft 63-9792, powered by TF33 turbofan engines, has a considerable number of antennas visible in this 14 April 1981 view of a low-level approach in the UK.
Peter R. Foster

In their second serious attempt to sell the E-3A Sentry to the RAF in late 1986, Boeing's sales people seemed to be pulling out all the stops. Speaking in London, Boeing vice-president Jerry King announced that the firm was increasing its controversial offer of contract offset work from 100% to 130%. King asserted that the 130% high-technology offset commitment would mean 50,000 British jobs over eight years, peaking at 8,000 new jobs per year. GEC Avionic's managing director Bill Alexander, supporting the Nimrod AEW3 (as well as an AWACS variant of the Lockheed C-130 Hercules), challenged these figures and pointed out that the Nimrod aircraft could begin service in 1987 while a RAF E-3A Sentry could not be delivered until 1989 or 1990. Alexander also used the export sales argument already mentioned. The campaign against buying Boeing culminated with GEC Avionics' full-page advertisement in the 27 November 1986 *Times* of London asserting that, even without export sales, Nimrod would secure 2,500 high technology jobs in Britain. Even Boeing acknowledged that only a scant 10% of its offset offer would involve the E-3As for the RAF, the remainder being indirect.

It was understood that Boeing was offering the RAF an aircraft similar to the Saudi KE-3A without the latter's secondary role as a tanker but with the 'fat' CFM56 engines. Boeing's original offer was for nine E-3As as compared with a GEC Avionics offer based on a force of 11 Nimrods. Upon drawing closer to the decision point, a package was put together taking into account the possibility that France might join with Britain in an AWACS buy. This seemed a case of wishful thinking. French intentions remained unclear at best and for once the difference between the KC-135 and the Boeing 707 seemed a disadvan-

Both will defend Britain. Only one will defend British industry.

In the coming weeks, Britain must choose between two airborne early warning systems.

Needless to say, the prime consideration in this debate is national security.

The Boeing AWACS system is already flying operationally.

But can the AEW Nimrod system deliver the goods?

The answer is emphatically "yes."

The entire radar system has been improved and upgraded.

And, in the words of one informed observer, these improvements now appear to be "a technical reality."

A further reality is that the AEW Nimrod can give the RAF an operational capability within twelve months.

This compares with three years for the Boeing AWACS system.

When it comes to the important area of total system costs, it is significant that the Boeing proposal has no advantage.

Indeed, despite the continuing debate about the millions invested so far, the AEW Nimrod will offer Britain a massive saving.

Which leaves us with one further major difference between the two systems.

Choosing the AEW Nimrod will defend the future of Britain's Avionics industry.

Choosing the Boeing AWACS will not.

For the past 30 years, GEC Avionics has been the mainstay of this high technology industry.

The Nimrod will allow this British success story to continue and secure 2,500 high technology jobs.

The fact is, GEC now offers the only airborne early warning capability outside the United States.

With seventeen nations, from France to China, already showing an interest, the export market has vast potential.

Proof positive that Britain needs the GEC Nimrod. **GEC AVIONICS**

Below:
E-3A Sentry 79-0449, alias LX-N90449, is seen at rest at Kleine Brogel, Belgium, on 28 June 1986, with various doors open and turbofan engines sheathed. For such a highly complex system, the E-3A has proven a most useful aircraft in front-line operational use. *Paul Bennett*

Left:
The E-3A AWACS v AEW Nimrod debate received high-profile coverage in the British press.
Times Newspapers

tage: a French E-3A even with CFM56 engines would have less than 40% compatibility with the C-135FR already used by *Armée de l'Air* (Chapter 7). With or without French participation, Jerry King insisted that a RAF E-3A would cost one-third less than Nimrod over the in-service life of the system, another figure which seemed difficult to prove but which made a sale sound attractive.

Arguments in favour of the Boeing product were also put forth by Ben P. Pamplin, the London-based vice-president of Westinghouse Defense International, which makes much of the electronic innards of the E-3A Sentry. 'The key point', argued Pamplin, 'is that an AEW system should provide the *earliest* possible warning of attack. The E-3A flies higher (than Nimrod), stays longer and looks farther'. Pamplin felt that the E-3A Sentry could provide as much as 10 minutes additional warning of such hostile threats as airbreathing cruise missiles. 'The key to this capability is the powerful and accurate Westinghouse radar . . . Boeing's 707 airframe was chosen so the radar and operating system design need not be compromised by airframe size and weight limitations unlike competing AEW systems. Continued performance improvements can be easily accommodated by the 707.'

Vulnerable

Precisely because it is unarmed and because it must be employed in wartime in direct support of combat operations, the E-3A Sentry is even more vulnerable to enemy counter-action than its KC-135 tanker cousin, which is, it should be said, vulnerable enough. One question never answered is how an AWACS aircraft would survive in a high-density combat situation of the kind which would attend a conflict between NATO and the Warsaw Pact. To fly 150 tons of metal at slow speed round and round in the sky while pumping out electronic signals is the surest way in today's world to *invite* enemy action.

Observers of big-aircraft operations are reminded of an instance just before the 1982 Falklands conflict when an Argentine Boeing 707 and a British Nimrod encountered each other in mid-air under hostile circumstances. Neither aircraft possessed a weapon to employ against the other! And, unlike the situation which would exist in a NATO/Warsaw Pact conflict, neither had supporting combat aircraft in the region. Unable to fight, the crews of the opposing aircraft merely signalled to each other and parted ways to fight another day.

So far, the E-3A Sentry has not been fitted with wingtip AIM-9 Sidewinders or other armament, nor is it believed that a fighter escort is regularly provided in US or NATO operations. But in an actual conflict, the likelihood of the AWACS becoming a sitting duck cannot be overlooked.

Below:
Because it has no dedicated tanker aircraft, the Soviet Union has no aircraft exactly comparable to the KC-135. For the AWACS' role filled by the E-3A Sentry, the Russians have put a rotodome atop the Tupolev Tu-126 'Moss', seen here, and the Ilyushin Il-86 'Mainstay'.
USN

Below:
KC-135A Stratotanker 62-3527 basks in brilliant sunlight in June 1976. *Douglas Barbier*

Right:
One of SAC's airborne command posts, this EC-135, 63-8057, is seen taking off from Hickam AFB, Hawaii, in the late 1960s. *Nicholas M. Williams*

Left:
**Typical of the Aeronautical
Systems Division's stable of test
aircraft is NKC-135A 55-3135 of
the ever-ubiquitous 4950th Test
Wing, seen at Edwards AFB,
California, on 12 November 1978.
The 18th Stratotanker built, this
'piccolo tube' has been through
several external changes over the
years.** *Nicholas M. Williams*

6 Command Post

When the idea of using the KC-135 as a flying command post was first put forth, it conjured up images of a post-Armageddon world in which the only humans left alive were SAC aircrews, led perhaps by a general like the Stirling Hayden character in *Doctor Strangelove*, winging through radioactive skies with no airbases to land at.

This vision could still become reality. Certainly, the vulnerability of fixed airfields is one area where the West needs to devote more attention. But it would have been foolhardy *not* to develop some kind of aerial platform manned with a battle staff under command of a general officer to function in a post-attack world. If airfields are vulnerable, so too are most military installations on the ground, including the National Military Command Center (NMCC) in the Pentagon and the alternate NMCC in a Virginia hillside. Only by assuring survival of some command and control functions can a nation claim preparedness in today's world. SAC's 'Looking Glass' operation, best known of the many command-post efforts by several commands, is as much a deterrent as its squadrons of B-1B bombers, proponents say.

The US Air Force's 1 July 1985 wrap-up of KC-135-related airframes in inventory listed no fewer than 10 different types of command posts ranging from six EC-135A 'Cover All' airframes to the EC-135Y assigned to the commander-in-chief of the US Central Command.

Illustrative of these is the EC-135A post-attack command and control system (PACCS) known as 'Looking Glass' which has operated continuously since 3 February 1961. Three aircraft per day, each on flights lasting eight hours or more, have kept a task commander, or Airborne Emergency Actions Officer (AEAO), aloft with his battle staff.

Initiated on a trial basis in July 1960, the system was proven after six months of evaluation. Ever since, the PACCS aircraft has remained aloft, able to communicate with the Joint Chiefs of Staff, any SAC base or any SAC aircraft on the ground or in the air. The first AEAO was Lt-Gen John P. McConnell, although the job is usually handled by an officer of brigadier-general rank. Until 25 March 1965 the PACCS force was operated by the 4363rd and 4364th Post Attack Command & Control Squadrons, located at Lockbourne AFB, Ohio (since renamed Rickenbacker AFB) and

Below:
The four EC-135Hs operated in Great Britain serve as airborne command posts for the US Commander-in-Chief Europe (USCINCEUR) who is also the NATO field commander. In a conflict they would be in secure communication with air, sea and land combat units. Aircraft 61-0285 is seen at RAF Fairford in 1985.
John Dunnell

Mountain Home AFB, Idaho, respectively. On the 1965 date, their radio-relay and other post-strike missions were absorbed by EC-135As that were assigned to the air refuelling squadrons at Lockbourne and Ellsworth AFB, South Dakota.

On 1 April 1970, SAC reorganised the PACCS operation again and moved some of its EC-135s out of Westover AFB, Massachusetts, Barksdale AFB, Louisiana, and March AFB, California. In this reorganisation, all EC-135s were assigned to the 2nd, 3rd and 4th Airborne Command & Control Squadrons, which were activated at Offutt AFB, Nebraska, Grissom AFB, Indiana, and Ellsworth. The mission remained the same, with 'Looking Glass' aircraft in the sky on a 24-hour basis. Auxiliary airborne command post and relay aircraft remained on round-the-clock ground alert.

Top:
Against a cloudy sky, wheels and flaps lowered, 61-0285 makes an approach. The EC-135H fleet might prove vulnerable in wartime, but seems to offer the best means yet devised to get a battlefield commander aloft and give him direct access to forces throughout a theatre.
Paul Bennett

Above:
Old aircraft, new engines. The first Stratotanker built (compare this with earlier photos), EC-135K 55-3118 became a command post while still equipped with the original J57 engines. Later, as seen here, it acquired TF33 turbofan engines. Aircraft 55-3118 serves with the 552nd Airborne Warning & Control Wing. *Paul Bennett*

NKC-135A test aircraft 55-3132 of the 4950th Test Wing, Aeronautical Systems Division, is stationed at Wright-Patterson AFB, Ohio, but was seen on a visit to RAF Mildenhall, England, on 22 March 1983. *Peter R. Foster*

The best known Presidential aircraft in the Boeing 707 series was VC-137C 62-6000, seen here at its Andrews AFB, Maryland, home on 12 December 1962. Eleven months later the aircraft was to bring the body of John F. Kennedy home from Dallas. *Major Robert C. Mikesh*

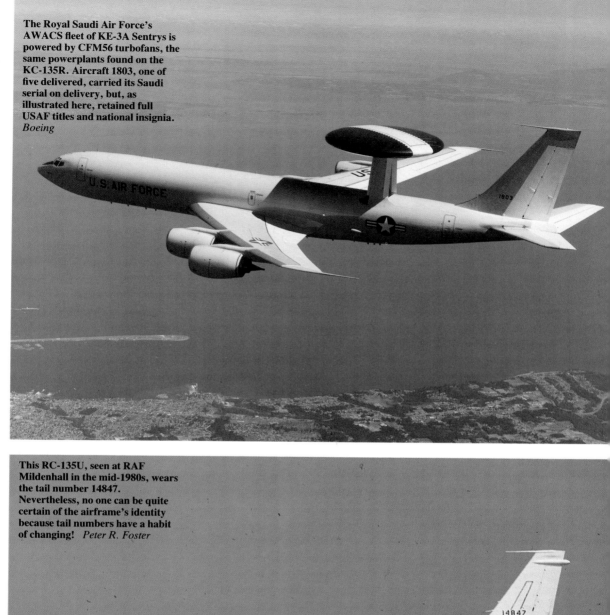

The Royal Saudi Air Force's AWACS fleet of KE-3A Sentrys is powered by CFM56 turbofans, the same powerplants found on the KC-135R. Aircraft 1803, one of five delivered, carried its Saudi serial on delivery, but, as illustrated here, retained full USAF titles and national insignia. *Boeing*

This RC-135U, seen at RAF Mildenhall in the mid-1980s, wears the tail number 14847. Nevertheless, no one can be quite certain of the airframe's identity because tail numbers have a habit of changing! *Peter R. Foster*

Above:
Aircraft 63-8054 had turbofan engines from the start, having been built as a KC-135B and subsequently converted to EC-135C standard. This SAC airborne command post is assigned to the 55th Strategic Reconnaissance Wing of Offutt AFB, Nebraska, where it is seen in May 1977. *Clyde Gerdes*

Below:
Seen on snow-covered terrain, 63-7994 is an EC-135G of the 305th Air Refueling Wing, Grissom AFB, Indiana, and is employed by SAC as an Airborne Launch Control Center (ALCC) for Minuteman ballistic missiles. Numerous blade antennae are located atop the fuselage of the Stratotanker. *USAF*

Bottom:
Seen in May 1966 at the outset of its career, EC-135H Stratotanker 61-0282 is still powered by its original J57 turbojet engines. The airborne command post operated by the 10th ACCS retains its fuelling boom and carries a six-mile trailing HF antenna which can be strung out behind the aircraft in flight. *Roger F. Besecker*

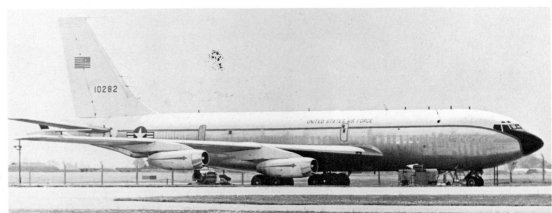

The notion of an airborne command post is recognition of the grim fact that the superpowers must prepare for nuclear war even while hoping to find ways to deter or prevent it. Many of the tools of nuclear war also have some conventional application — long-range bombers can carry conventional as well as atomic bombs, for example — but in the case of the command post, it is almost impossible to visualise the aircraft in use without also seeing a clear picture of the holocaust nobody wants.

A trans-polar nuclear conflict might begin with heavy megaton hydrogen weapons being exploded at high altitude to barrage the United States with invisible blasts of electromagnetic pulse (EMP). These unseen electronic gremlins might well throw out of commission almost every electronic device, computer or piece of communications equipment which is not hardened against them. With American command, control and communications then blasted asunder, intercontinental missiles might be directed against the surviving command centres which could direct the US war effort, including SAC headquarters at Offutt. No such command centre, not even the much-publicised North American defence centre in Cheyene Mountain, Colorado, is invulnerable to a direct hit by a large-megaton warhead. In a worst case situation, all or most command centres on the ground would become useless, leaving the Stratotanker command post as the surviving national authority. SAC planners believe that readiness for this situation is exactly what is needed to prevent it.

To refer once again to the US Air Force's Tinker Report, variants which carry out the airborne command post mission include the following:

● **EC-135A** is the designation covering six KC-135A tankers which were modified in 1965. One of these was subsequently returned to tanker configuration, leaving five in inventory:

Serial No	Engine	Used by
61-262	J57-P-59	28th BMW/Ellsworth AFB, South Dakota
61-278	J57-P-59	28th BMW/Ellsworth AFB, South Dakota
61-287	J57-P-59	28th BMW/Ellsworth AFB, South Dakota
61-289	J57-P-59	28th BMW/Ellsworth AFB, South Dakota
61-297	J57-P-59	28th BMW/Ellsworth AFB, South Dakota

These aircraft have Airborne Launch Control Center (ALCC) equipment and special communications equipment for use in the World Wide Airborne Command Post (WWABNCP) programme. The launch equipment is understood to enable the general officer aboard an EC-135A to effect the launch of land-based intercontinental ballistic missiles under certain conditions. This, of course, points to the core of the aircraft's mission,

as described in a SAC history: to take command of the surviving elements of the SAC aircraft and missile forces in the event that Headquarters SAC and other ground-based alternate command headquarters were destroyed or unable to make contact with these forces. One measure of how well the command post role is performed is that during its first 15 years of continuous operation, the command post aircraft flew 16,078 sorties and 149,600 accident-free hours.

The 'Looking Glass' or 'Cover All' EC-135As are equipped to receive in-flight refuelling in order to remain on station in a post-strike situation. In theory they would be able to stay aloft until the oil in their engines was depleted after about 72 hours of continuous flight. In any real doomsday situation, however, it is likely that tankers to provide the in-flight refuelling would be depleted before engine oil. At this late stage in the programme, it seems remarkable that these command posts still rely on the old 'water-burning' engines when most other special variants of the basic aircraft have more up-to-date powerplants.

● **EC-135B** is the designation for a single aircraft which is not precisely a command post and which, in any event, was being modified in 1985 for a new role.

Serial No	Engine	Used by
62-4128	TF33-P-5	Air Force Logistics Command

Originally delivered as a C-135B, this aircraft was modified into a Telemetry/Range Instrument Aircraft assigned to Air Force Systems Command and operated out of Patrick AFB, Florida, providing communication support for the space programme. It was later modified into the Apollo/Advanced Range Instrumented Aircraft (ARIA) configuration using equipment removed from an EC-135N aircraft. In 1978-79 it was modified to EC-135B standard. According to the Air Force report, 62-4128 was to be modified to RC-135X standard to join the SAC reconnaissance fleet, although no details of the RC-135X configuration are known.

● **EC-135C** is the designation for the principal command post aircraft which carry out the 'Looking Glass' function of putting an alternate SAC command staff into the air. The Tinker Report listed 13 such aircraft:

Serial No	Engine	Used by
62-3581	TF33-P9	55th SRW/Offutt AFB, Nebraska,
62-3582	TF33-P9	28th BMW/Ellsworth AFB, South Dakota

From starboard, C-135A
Stratolifter 62-3558 was seen at
Hickam in about May 1969.
Nicholas M. Williams

Serial No	Engine	Used by
62-3583	TF33-P9	55th SRW/Offutt AFB, Nebraska
62-3585	TF33-P9	55th SRW/Offutt AFB, Nebraska
63-8046	TF33-P9	55th SRW/Offutt AFB, Nebraska
63-8047/8048	TF33-P9	28th BMW/Ellsworth AFB, South Dakota
63-8049/8050	TF33-P9	55th SRW/Offutt AFB, Nebraska
63-8051	TF33-P9	28th BMW/Ellsworth AFB, South Dakota
63-8052/8054	TF33-P9	55th SRW/Offutt AFB, Nebraska

These were originally delivered as part of the 17 KC-135B aircraft purchased, and all 17 were modified to EC-135C standard for the 'Looking Glass' mission. Four aircraft have since been modified to EC-135J configuration.

These command post aircraft are, of course, equipped to receive in-flight refuelling.

● **EC-135G** is the term for the command post aircraft which are actually intended to take over the job of launching Minuteman intercontinental missiles from the missile fields in the north-central United States. The Air Force inventory totalled four airframes, as follows:

Serial No	Engine	Used by
62-3570	J57-P-59	28th BMW/Ellsworth AFB, South Dakota
62-3579	J57-P-59	28th BMW/Ellsworth AFB, South Dakota
63-7994	J57-P-59	305th AREFW/Grissom AFB, Indiana,
63-8001	J57-P-59	28th BMW/Ellsworth AFB, South Dakota

Again, given their post-strike role, it is not surprising that these aircraft, too, are equipped to receive in-flight refuelling. These are Airborne Launch Control Center (ALCC) relay link aircraft.

● **EC-135H** is the terminology covering command post aircraft assigned to Tactical Air Command (TAC) and US Air Forces in Europe (USAFE), and performing for those commands essentially the same job as other command posts carry out for SAC. Five of these are listed in inventory:

Serial No	Engine	Used by
61-274	TF33-P-102	6 ACCS/Langley AFB, Virginia

Serial No	Engine	Used by
61-282	TF33-P-102	10 ACCS/RAF Mildenhall, UK
61-285/286	TF33-P-102	10 ACCS/RAF Mildenhall, UK
61-291	TF33-P-102	10 ACCS/RAF Mildenhall, UK

The first EC-135H, 61-274, is assigned to the 'Scope Light' programme to support the Commander-in-Chief Atlantic. The remaining four airframes are assigned to the 'Silk Purse' programme to support the US field commander in Europe who is, of course, also the NATO commander. All five are equipped to be refuelled in flight.

● **EC-135J** is the command post employed in the Pacific to keep the US commander-in-chief in that region (CINCPAC) ready for crisis. The inventory listing for this designation shows four machines in service:

Serial No	Engine	Used by
62-3584	TF33-P-9	9 ACCS/Hickam AFB, Hawaii
63-8055/8057	TF33-P-9	9 ACCS/Hickam AFB, Hawaii

Three EC-135C aircraft were converted to EC-135J in 1965-66, while a fourth (62-3584) was converted in February 1980. These aircraft had been used by the National Command Authority, meaning the Pentagon, under the 'Night Watch' programme until 1975 when they were transferred to the present 'Blue Eagle' mission, providing aerial command post support for CINCPAC. Again, the aircraft are equipped to receive air refuelling.

● **EC-135K** is another designation for a Tactical Air Command aircraft. Two of these machines remained in the inventory listing:

Serial No	Engine	Used by
55-3118	TF33-P-102	522nd AW&CW/Tinker AFB, Oklahoma
59-1518	TF33-P-102	522nd AW&CW/Tinker AFB, Oklahoma

Three aircraft were originally converted to this standard, one (52-3536) having been lost in September 1977. It is noteworthy that the first of the survivors, 55-3118, was the prototype

Top:
EC-135H 61-0291 is another member of the 'Silk Purse' command post fleet based in England with the 10th ACCS. This view shows the aircraft in 1979 with a black nose. *John Dunnell*

Above:
Another view of 61-0291, taken after the nose was painted white and the J57 turbojet engines had been replaced by TF33 turbofans. *Paul Bennett*

Below:
Another early view of a command post. EC-135H 61-0285 is seen in 1979 before its black nose radome was painted white and before the J57 turbojets were replaced by TF33 turbofans. The white protrusion under the fuselage at the wing joint is the retractable HF radio antenna which can trail for six miles behind the aircraft in flight. *John Dunnell*

KC-135A and has been in continuous service, being far too valuable for retirement to a museum! This machine was of course re-engined in addition to acquiring the command post role. S/n 59-1518 had previously been employed for tests by the Federal Aviation Administration (FAA) and thereafter had been in temporary storage until 1979.

The two airframes in the EC-135K series serve as Tactical Deployment & Control Aircraft (TDCA) during aircraft movements. Their wing in Oklahoma is of course the same wing which operates the E-3A Sentry AWACS aircraft.

● **EC-135L** is yet another in the seemingly interminable roster of designations for flying command posts, this referring to additional machines in the SAC 'Cover All' programme. The inventory listing identifies five:

Serial No	Engine	Used by
61-261	J57-P-59	305th AREFW/Grissom AFB, Indiana
61-263	J57-P-59	305th AREFW/Grissom AFB, Indiana
61-269	J57-P-59	305th AREFW/Grissom AFB, Indiana
61-279	J57-P-59	305th AREFW/Grissom AFB, Indiana
61-283	J57-P-59	305th AREFW/Grissom AFB, Indiana

Eight KC-135As were converted to EC-135Ls in 1965. Five are still in service as radio relay aircraft, part of the PACCS network. Three others (61-288, 61-302, 62-281) were returned to KC-135A tanker configuration.

These aircraft are used as relay aircraft and serve as part of the PACCS network. They have special communications systems, Airborne Launch Control Center equipment and other related systems. They too are equipped to receive air-to-air refuelling.

● **EC-135P** is the appellation for aircraft operated by Tactical Air Command in support of the Atlantic forces commander (CINCLANT). They would work in co-ordination with the sole EC-135H assigned for the same purpose. The roster lists three surviving airframes:

Serial No	Engine	Used by
55-3129	TF33-P-102	6 ACCS/Langley AFB, Virginia
58-019	TF33-P-102	6 ACCS/Langley AFB, Virginia
58-022	TF33-P-102	6 ACCS/Langley AFB, Virginia

Five tanker aircraft originally were assigned to the 'Looking Glass' mission and were converted to EC-135P configuration in 1966-67. One of these, 58-007, was lost in a ground fire in January 1980. Two others, 58-001 and 58-018, were converted back to the tanker configuration. This left 58-019 and 58-022 from the original batch, and they were joined by 55-3129 which was converted to an EC-135P from NKC-135A standard in June 1984.

These aircraft form yet another component of the worldwide airborne command post system and are assigned under the 'Scope Light' programme to function as flying command posts for CINCLANT. They are equipped to be refuelled in flight.

● **EC-135Y** is the term covering a one-off communications and support aircraft assigned to the US Army Central Command and operated for the Army by a SAC crew. One aircraft is listed:

Serial No	Engine	Used by
55-3125	J57-P-59	19th AREFW/Robins AFB, Georgia

This machine brings to an end the list of Air Force Stratotankers converted to function as command posts. This airframe was originally delivered as a KC-135A. It was used for test purposes for a number of years by Air Force Systems Command and was redesignated NKC-135A. It was declared excess to that command's needs in 1983 and was modified to EC-135Y standard in early 1984.

The aircraft is stationed at its Georgia location to meet the communications and operational support needs of the chief of Army Central Command (CINCENT). A second phase in the modification of the aircraft for this role had not been completed as of 1 July 1985 and this additional work was scheduled for 1986-87.

With all of these command posts winging about in American skies, it is perhaps appropriate to note that no *Doctor Strangelove* scenario can realistically occur. As with all other components of the US nuclear deterrent, the airborne command posts operate under stringent controls. In the case of the Airborne Launch Control Center (ALCC) aircraft which are equipped to fire intercontinental missiles, the system must first be activated by the aircraft commander, who must be satisfied that a valid emergency message has been received. He then switches on the system. ALCC safeguards still require two key turns for launch orders to be issued. One key is held by the general officer aboard the aircraft, the other by the communications officer. These two sit at opposite ends of the battle staff compartment. As with land-based launch centres, this arrangement is intended to prevent accidental or unauthorised launch of nuclear missiles.

The literature of atomic warfare makes it clear that in recent years both the US and the Soviet Union have studied a kind of conflict which might fall short of a global holocaust, which some strategists believe could be 'won' by their side, and which would include nuclear strikes both against offensive weapons systems and, more importantly, against the command, control, communications and intelligence capabilities (C^3I) of the opposing side. A reckless Soviet decision to embark on such a conflict — probably as unthinkable to Moscow as to Washington, but part of military thinking nonetheless — would mean nuclear attacks on the nerve centres of the American war machine. Facilities such as the National Military Command Center in the Pentagon, SAC headquarters at Offutt AFB, Nebraska, and Tactical Air Command headquarters at Langley AFB, Virginia, would certainly come under assault during any such 'decapitation' strikes. Destruction of these facilities and the deaths of key leaders, such as the President, the Secretary of Defense and the SAC commander, would be an attempt to immobilise the US defence apparatus by, in effect, lopping off its head. The presence of airborne command posts, to provide a continuity of leadership, could thus be a more important weapon than any missile or bomber.

It has already been noted that airborne command posts could be vulnerable to EMP (electromagnetic pulse), the withering blast of energy which would come from explosion of multi-megaton nuclear weapons in the atmosphere at high altitude. Critics of US defence readiness have also charged that the long trailing antenna unreeled from an EC-135 command post can snap off during a turn, leaving the aircraft with no working communications. Serious efforts have been made to redress these kinds of problems, and the flying command posts have more than proven themselves over the years.

Another 'E' Plane

Just as the command posts help to assure the effectiveness of the land-based portion of the US strategic force (its ICBMs and bombers) another kind of flying staff centre is intended to assure the survivability and effectiveness of US ballistic missile submarines (SSBN). Based upon the Model 707 airliner rather than the KC-135 tanker, the Boeing E-6A is intended to take over a US Navy mission called TACAMO, an acronym for Take Charge & Move Out. This mission, operated now by Lockheed EC-130G and EC-130Q Hercules, is designed to guarantee survivable communications to the submerged SSBN force, to prevent the force from being out of touch with national leaders. One aircraft is kept on patrol over the Atlantic and a second over the Pacific. Like some of the SAC command posts, these aircraft pull a 6.2-mile (10km) trailing antenna and communicate with submarines via VLF radio.

The US Navy plans to acquire 15 E-6A aircraft to replace the Hercules fleet. Cost of the package was estimated several years ago at $2 billion (thousand million), almost certainly a conservative figure. The aircraft will be converted Boeing 707-320B airliners, re-engined with the increasingly familiar 'fat' GE/SNECMA CFM56 turbofan which has the military designation F108-CF-100. A recognition feature of the E-6A will be bulky wingtip pods containing VLF trailing antennae. The E-6A's range of 6,900 miles (11,200km), together with its capability of being refuelled in flight, makes it another candidate to remain aloft for an extended duration at the outset of any conflict. Just as SAC's flying command post can fill in for ground-based command centres, the E-6A can take over for the Navy's important but highly vulnerable submarine communications sites. The E-6A aircraft will be fitted with special-mission electronics and hardened against EMP. Faint hearts need not apply to join the elite crews who will man these aircraft, it appears: a typical patrol in the E-6A may take as long as 14 hours, the men packed together inside a cramped windowless tube of a fuselage, and under extreme conditions the time spent aloft could be much more.

At the end of 1986, after surviving numerous threats from cost-conscious legislators, the E-6A programme appeared to face serious funding difficulties with a deficit-conscious Congress scrutinising every line item in the defence budget. The familiar question of vulnerability also arises with the E-6A, even though it might operate at considerable distance from an enemy's main forces; hardpoints on the wing will accommodate chaff dispensers while mountings and wiring will be fitted in the wings for future ECM gear and possibly Sidewinders. Given the critical importance of flying command posts, it has to be assumed that the funding will continue and that the E-6A programme will forge ahead as scheduled.

7 Ravitailleur

For so successful an aircraft, the Stratotanker had almost no export orders. Of the 820 airframes in the Boeing KC-135 Stratotanker family, a mere 12 have served outside the US armed forces. Their role has been to support an independent French strategic force about which, ironically, the United States has had mixed feelings at best. The French word *Ravitailleur* (tanker) describes the principal role filled by these machines, which also double as cargo and passenger carriers.

In the mid-1960s, France set forth to develop its own nuclear force and quickly decided that the Mirage IV bomber would be a key ingredient of that force. If the Mirage IV was to reach targets in the Soviet Union, in-flight refuelling tankers would have to be acquired together with the bombers. The decision to purchase Boeing tankers more or less coincided with the January 1964 founding of France's equivalent of SAC, the *Forces Aériennes Stratégiques*, and with the first French detonation of a nuclear weapon which followed in October of that year.

Col Claude Rossello, France's air attaché in London and a C-135F pilot for 14 years, points out that *Armée de l'Air's* decision to purchase

12 C-135F aircraft (63-8470/8475; 63-12735/12740) involved a number of choices and compromises: 'We got almost everything we wanted for the right price.' Ideally, the French would have preferred a turbofan-powered variant, but they settled on the ubiquitous water-burning J57 engines — smoke-strewn exhaust trails and all — because with this powerplant a lesser up-front expenditure was needed.

In another kind of compromise, France acquired airframes which had a dual capability of air transport and air refuelling, and therefore had two pressurised lobes in the fuselage rather than one as on the American KC-135A. The principal purpose was always to have a tanker force, and the tanker force was always primary, but the absence of a 'K'

Below:
The C-135F combination tanker/transport was essential to France's development of an independent *Forces Aériennes Stratégiques*. In its original configuration with J57 turbojet engines, a C-135F is seen refuelling a Mirage IV. *Marcel Dassault*

Above:
C-135F Stratotanker 312738 in flight with a Jaguar receiver aircraft en route to Libreville, Gabon, during a 1981 deployment. France received 12 C-135F aircraft, as shown here, originally powered by J57 engines, and one was lost in a mishap over the western Pacific. *ECPA*

(for tanker) from the C-135F designation reflects the secondary function which the C-135F has performed ably over the years, hauling supplies and cargo and people from Metropolitan France to one global outpost after another.

The first C-135F was delivered in February 1964 to the French air base at Istres, which is the home of the French C-135 community. Located at Istres is a wing command, one of three C-135F squadrons (1/93 *Escadron de Ravitaillement en Vol*), an operational conversion unit (OCU), and a second-line maintenance facility. The remaining squadrons are at Avord (2-93) and at Mont-de-Marsan (3/93). Deliveries of the C-135F were completed by July 1965. The first fully operational squadron was the one at Mont-de-Marsan in October 1964, and the wing was considered fully operational as of early 1966.

Professional Crews

To fly the C-135F, the French air arm uses only pilots who have already acquired 1,500 hours and

puts them through a strict regimen before turning them loose. Col Rossello, who went from junior co-pilot to wing commander, points out that the C-135F is not the most forgiving aircraft in the world. 'Even well-qualified pilots are surprised at how difficult the 135 can be in a crosswind', Rossello says. 'It is a good aircraft to fly, but it is sometimes difficult. It is hard to handle in a roll. On final approach for a landing, the C-135F is as fast as a fighter.'

French crews use the American 'Dash One' (flight manual), which is available only in the English language. The water-injection J57 engines can be an annoyance to French airmen, since the C-135F must use a mineral-free water. Any other kind would damage the compressor. The water-injection engines can use up to 5,000lb (2,277kg) of fuel on a typical take-off. This feature of the aircraft has been especially difficult for French crews in tropical locations like Chad or Tahiti, particularly those locations where pure water is not always readily available. It is also worth noting that when employed in the transport role, the C-135F is difficult to load and unload, especially in primitive locations. The C-135F cannot be refuelled in flight.

That said, the C-135F has had a remarkable record with the French air force, having logged about 170,000 flying hours and 200,000 in-flight refuellings. Each aircraft flies about 700 hours a

Below:
A C-135F transport/tanker of France's *Armée de l'Air* with J57 engines and probe and drogue refuelling system, seen on a visit to the UK. *Peter R. March*

Bottom:
A Mirage 2000 with two MATRA Magic and two MATRA Super 530 missiles is refuelled from a French tanker. The lettering on the boom says 'High Speed Boom'. *Service Press GIFAS*

year and had flown 12,000 hours by the mid-1980s when a decision was made to embark on a re-engining programme.

New Engines

The superb record has been marred by only one aircraft loss. This occurred in June 1972, when C-135F 63-8473 with Maj Georges DuGué and his crew vanished on a flight over the South Pacific. There was no emergency call for help, and the cause of the loss has never been determined. The C-135F went down in waters considered too deep for practical salvage.

In 1977-79, in a programme similar to one embarked upon by the US Air Force, the remaining 11 C-135Fs were re-skinned at the Boeing Military Airplane Co, Wichita, Kansas. Some of the re-skinned aircraft have now accumulated as many as 17,000 to 18,000 flight hours, and Col Rossello explains that Armée de l'Air intends to keep the aircraft type in service until 2005.

To make this possible, France belatedly embarked on a very ambitious programme to upgrade and re-engine its 11 C-135Fs. In 1985-86 all 11 airframes were re-engined with the CFM56-2-B1, known to the US military as F108-CF-100, the massive fanjet engine which is also being retrofitted to the US Air Force KC-135R. The French aircraft became known as

C-135FR upon completion of this upgrade. The new engines develop up to 20,000lb (8,060kg) of static thrust and eliminate the need for water injection.

The French tankers can employ either the flying boom or probe and drogue refuelling system. Aircraft which have been refuelled by the C-135F in French service include the Mirage IV (since 1964), F-100 Super Sabre (1964-75), Jaguar (since 1975), Mirage F1 (since 1978) and Mirage 2000 (since 1983). Presumably any new French military aircraft design, such as an operational version of the Rafale fighter demonstrated so dramatically at Farnborough in 1986, would be equipped to accept mid-air refuelling from the present-day C-135FR.

Despite the excellent record for safety and reliability established by France's tanker force, the total of 11 airframes remains a tiny figure. Like their counterparts in the US Air Force, French tactical aviators wonder if air refuelling will be available for them in time of actual conflict. As with the US forces, the first priority for air refuelling goes to the strategic air arm. Whether anything will be left over for the shorter-range tactical aircraft also participating in the conflict remains to be seen.

As in the US services, the C-135FR is operated with a crew of four consisting of aircraft commander, second pilot, navigator and boom operator. A typical mission might begin with a pre-dawn take-off and a flight of as much as 600 miles (960km) to a predetermined air refuelling control point. If the endurance of the tanker itself is not at issue, the mission may be flown in a lo-hi profile, with the tanker climbing to around 12,000ft (3,657m) only in time for the refuelling rendezvous. Over the thickly-populated plains of Europe where a SAM or Triple-A threat can materialise at any time, even an unarmed tanker must remain as low as possible and the French crews have practised flying as low as 500ft (152m). Rehearsing for wartime, the C-135FR might return to its base via a wholly different route and at a different speed and altitude. A realistic refuelling mission in which wartime circumstances are simulated may take from four to eight hours and test every aspect of the crew's flying skill right up to the limit. Many missions are, of course, far more routine and are flown merely to accomplish an immediate goal rather than to simulate the conditions of a NATO/Warsaw Pact conflict.

Col Rossello feels that the venerable French C-135FR with its new engines and old airframe can probably keep 'right on flying, forever and ever'. This is a bit of an exaggeration but the year 2005 *is* a realistic date for the end of the story and 35,000 hours seems a possible figure for each individual airframe.

Below:
France has put its 11 surviving Stratotankers through an exhaustive upgrading programme which included re-engining with CFM56 turbofans. The aircraft are now designated C-135FR. *French Air Force*

8 Combatant

A bright future and a long career must have seemed on the cards for Boeing's remarkable tanker from the moment the tenth machine, 55-3127, was delivered to the 93rd Air Refueling Squadron at Castle AFB, California, to begin the type's operational service. 'We *knew*', says Sgt Steve Huxley, a boom operator, 'from the very beginning when the 135 went operational, we *knew* it was going to be a great aircraft with a great future.' Less evident at the time was the plain fact that the KC-135A was going to have to go to war. But a war did lie ahead, and, inevitably, the KC-135A was to be a participant.

Gen LeMay liked the KC-135A. To a generation of Air Force officers, many of whom sought in vain to persuade the cigar-smoking LeMay that fighters were almost as important as bombers, any hint of favour from the tough-minded, thoroughly dedicated LeMay was regarded as a treasure. And although he had left his command of SAC to become Vice-Chief of Staff, LeMay did not merely indicate that he favoured the aeroplane: he flew it.

On 11 and 12 November 1957, Gen Curtis E. LeMay, at the controls of the ninth aircraft delivered, 55-3126, established an official world record on a non-stop, unrefuelled flight of 6,322.85 miles (8,315.26km) from Westover AFB, Massachusetts, to Buenos Aires, Argentina. Total flying time was 13hr 1min 51sec. By flying around the hump of Brazil, Gen LeMay added approximately 1,000 miles (1,609km) to the direct airline distance from Westover to Buenos Aires. For this record flight the General was awarded the Harmon International Trophy.

On 7/8 April 1958, another KC-135A Stratotanker (aircraft 56-3601) of the 93rd Air Refueling Squadron, Fairchild AFB, Washington, established these world records: distance in a straight line without refuelling, 10,229.3 miles (16,366.88km), Tokyo to Lajes, Azores; speed 492.262mph (787.61km/hr), Tokyo to Washington DC in 13hr 45min 46.5sec. The KC-135A was piloted by Brig-Gen William E. Eubank, 93rd Bomb Wing commander.

'Top Sail' Record Flight
On 27-29 June 1958, two KC-135As from the 99th Air Refueling Squadron broke the existing speed records in flights from New York to London and return. The actual records established by the lead aircraft (56-3830), piloted by Maj Burn B. Davenport, were as follows: New York to London, 5hr 29min 14.64sec; London to New York, 5hr 53min 12.77sec. (The flights, code-named 'Top Sail', originated at Westover AFB, Massachusetts.)

A third KC-135A (56-3599), scheduled to participate in the flight, crashed on take-off at Westover on 25 June 1958. Among the 15 men killed were Brig-Gen Donald W. Saunders, 57th Air Division commander, and Lt-Col George M. Broutsas, 99th Air Refueling Squadron commander. Thus 56-3599 became the second KC-135A to crash, having been preceded by 56-3598 on 25 March 1958. Still, a series of most impressive records had been racked up. Few aircraft types had entered service and achieved so much.

This was only the beginning. On 17 September 1958, Capt Charles E. Gibbs, flying a KC-135A of the 92nd Air Refueling Squadron, also based at Fairchild AFB, Washington, established four world records: distance in a closed circuit without refuelling, 3,125.56 miles (5,030.4km); speed for 2.00km (1.24 miles), 589.278mph (948.348km/hr), closed circuit with 2,204.6lb, 4,409.2lb, 11,023lb and 22,046lb payloads (1,000kg, 2,000kg, 4,000kg and 8,000kg payloads); speed for 5,000km (3,106.86 miles), 587.136mph (994.9km/hr); and closed circuit with the same payloads. The KC-135A had embarked on its service career with a remarkable set of achievements.

Until the advent of the KC-135A, air refuelling aircraft had been assigned to various major commands such as Pacific Air Forces (PACAF), Tactical Air Command (TAC), and US Air Forces in Europe (USAFE). Each of these, for example, had its own complement of Boeing KB-50J Superfortress tankers. In November 1961, however, Headquarters USAF determined that SAC should be the sole manager of all KC-135A fuelling operations. It was decided that the KC-135A programme would comprise 32 squadrons, with 20 aircraft per squadron. SAC would provide in-flight refuelling to the other commands but they would lose their own tankers, leaving the refuelling function in the same hands as the strategic warfare mission.

The conflict in South-East Asia was growing. In the 1959-61 period, small numbers of American advisors were sent to South Vietnam to help that country in its struggle against Viet Cong insurgency. The first US Air Force personnel in Vietnam flew vintage T-28 and B-26 aircraft, but it soon became apparent that more advanced warplanes would be needed in the growing conflict. The first US Air Force *unit* to reach the combat zone was the 15th Tactical Reconnaissance Squadron, nicknamed the 'Cotton Pickers', which set up shop with its RF-101C Voodoos at Saigon's Tan Son Nhut airport in early 1961.

Widening War

With only a few hundred Americans scattered around South Vietnam and the war virtually unknown to the public back home, Voodoo pilots at Tan Son Nhut were more concerned with primitive conditions than with enemy gunfire. At one point, airport authorities announced that there was no JP4 fuel. To keep the Voodoos flying, the Air Force brought in KB-50J Superfortress tankers which proceeded to refuel the RF-101Cs *while sitting on the ground*. The KB-50J was too slow and vulnerable for use in combat — indeed, the notion of using *any* tanker aircraft on combat missions was still a premature idea — but on occasion the Voodoos linked up with US Navy A4D-2N Skyhawks equipped with 'buddy' refuelling packages. With a gradual build-up under way, with F-100 and F-105 fighters moving into friendly bases in Thailand, a need for the KC-135A was readily apparent, especially if the war was going to continue to escalate.

In those early days, the reconnaissance and fighter forces were directed against operations by the communist Pathet Lao forces in Laos, which were being supported directly by the Soviet Union. On 9 June 1964, SAC tankers were used to support combat efforts in South-East Asia for the first time. Four KC-135A Stratotankers, flying out of Clark Air Base in the Philippines and nicknamed Yankee Team Tanker Task Force, refuelled eight F-100 Super Sabres on their way to strike Pathet Lao anti-aircraft emplacements in the Plain of Jars in southern Laos. The tankers loitered over southern Laos until the strike was over and then

refuelled two of the fighters before returning to Clark.

These tankers eventually returned to their home at Andersen Air Base, Guam, but two months later, on 5 August 1964, the Joint Chiefs of Staff re-established the Yankee Team Tanker Task Force at Clark. Consisting of eight KC-135As and re-named Foreign Legion on 3 September 1964, this task force began supporting fighters engaged in combat in Laos, beginning 28 September.

A turning point in the South-East Asia conflict had come on the night of 2 August 1964 when North Vietnamese torpedo boats attacked the destroyer USS *Maddox* in coastal waters. A second attack may have taken place on 4 August when *Maddox* was joined by USS *Turner Joy*. The destroyers were on an intelligence-gathering mission which Hanoi could have considered a provocation, but in the wake of the attack on the ships it was Lyndon Johnson who became provoked. On 5 August 1964, US Navy aircraft flew strikes against targets in North Vietnam in retaliation. Americans debated, actively and publicly, whether to begin bombing North Vietnam on a sustained basis.

By 20 October 1965, Headquarters USAF had decided to commit a force of 10 KC-135As to South-East Asia, a step which was viewed with urgency because the high-hour KB-50J tankers were being phased out of service more rapidly than anticipated. Public debate continued over the possibility of launching a sustained aerial campaign against North Vietnam, and it was evident that tankers would be needed for any such effort. On 1 December 1964, Col Morgan S. Tyler Jr led a SAC team to Thailand to decide on a forward operating base. Kadena AB, Okinawa, had already been selected as the main base for KC-135 operations in the Pacific and Tyler quickly chose

Bangkok's Don Muang airport as the forward base.

By January 1965 the KC-135 effort in South-East Asia had acquired yet another nickname 'Young Tiger'. This was the term for KC-135As arriving at Kadena to fulfil the mission of the 4252nd Strategic Wing, which was activated on 12 January. Already, plans were germinating to employ B-52 bombers in South Vietnam, on missions which would be given the name 'Arc Light'. Tyler started from scratch in setting up the wing on Okinawa, beginning with six officers and 22 airmen, and soon the Kadena base was in a state of chaos with as many as 30 tankers abruptly on strength.

Foreign Legion, the KC-135A task force at Clark Field in the Philippines, ended its six-tanker operation on 1 March 1965 and resumed operations 12 hours later at Don Muang as the Tiger Cub Tanker Task Force. These KC-135As served fighter-bombers stationed in Thailand.

They were needed sooner than anyone expected. On 2 March 1965 President Johnson launched the 'Rolling Thunder' campaign against North Vietnam, a sustained effort aimed at choking off the flow of military supplies to communist insurgents in the south. On 18 June

1965, 'Arc Light' bombing operations began with the first B-52 strike in South Vietnam. Although the first strike was less than a success — two B-52s collided in mid-air and all men aboard both bombers were killed — it was clear that the US was now embarked on a major air war and that air refuelling would be a vital part of it. By mid-1965 there were no fewer than 45 tankers at Kadena sustaining combat operations. Tyler's small group of temporary-duty people had become one of the largest wings in the Air Force.

Combat Operations
The sight of F-4C Phantoms or F-105 Thunderchiefs, laden with bombs and clinging to the tanker's boom to take on fuel, soon became all too familiar. On a typical strike against barracks, rail lines and bridges in the area around Hanoi known as Route Package Six, a formation of eight Thunderchiefs would rendezvous with a pair of tankers at an air refuelling control point over Thailand, top off their fuel tanks and proceed into North Vietnam with enough fuel to loiter in the target area if necessary.

On 15 September 1965 the first three KC-135As of what was called the King Cobra Task Force began to fly refuelling sorties from yet another new location, Takhli airbase in Thailand. Similar to the tanker force located at Don Muang, this component eventually numbered as many as 15 Stratotankers, although the facilities at Takhli were far from optimum. All fuel used at Takhli had to be trucked from Bangkok, an expensive and cumbersome arrangement.

In fact, just about every aspect of KC-135A operations in South-East Asia was more difficult than anyone had foreseen. At one point the King Cobra maintenance facility at Takhli was a one-room, ramshackle wooden structure without the air conditioning which became commonplace later in the conflict. With a force that grew to 55 tankers by 1966, of which 30 were committed to 'Arc Light' operations, SAC people began to encounter a variety of maintenance and support problems. Completion of yet another airfield at U-Tapao, Thailand, was long-delayed and it was not until 11 August 1966 that U-Tapao's 10-tanker force, named Giant Cobra, was in operation. On that date, Col H. L. Holley flew the first mission from U-Tapao with aircraft 59-1489 of the 919th Air Refueling Squadron. By now a furious air war was raging over North Vietnam, with Thunderchiefs and Phantoms facing Hanoi's formidable anti-aircraft, missile and MiG defences, and the tankers were at work around the clock.

The intrepid SAC tanker crews, often given little credit in the press, began to compile a remarkable record of 'saves' of tactical aircraft which otherwise would have been lost in the

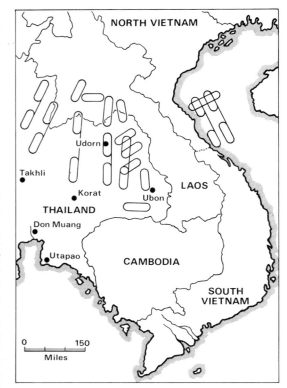

conflict. It was not uncommon for a damaged Phantom or Thunderchief, leaking fuel furiously, to be 'towed' by a KC-135 until a sufficient fuel supply could be assured to permit a return to base.

On 5 July 1966 a flight of four F-105s got into a typical point-blank air battle with MiG-17s and exhausted their fuel much faster than expected. Reacting to their emergency, a tanker headed for them at maximum speed. When the tanker arrived, the F-105s had as little as 200lb (86kg) of fuel remaining in their tanks. Two of the pilots had already decided to eject but were persuaded to attempt a last-minute hook-up. The tanker mated firstly with the number four F-105, which by then had less than 100lb (44kg) of fuel in its tanks. The F-105 pilot was in such a plight that he made the hook-up in a left-hand 30° bank and took on just enough fuel to keep going. By this time, the lead F-105 pilot was looking at an 'empty' fuel gauge and quickly moved in to take on a token load. In a kind of leap-frog arrangement, the KC-135A crew kept skipping from one F-105 to another, until all four aircraft had enough fuel to maintain flight and could then accept a full load with greater leisure. Four happy fighter pilots owed their survival to a KC-135A of the 301st Air Refueling Squadron piloted by Capt Howard G. Stalnecker.

Other remarkable saves entered the SAC record books, including the 3 May 1967 mission by

Left:
BUF on the boom. In the Eleven Day War of 18-29 December 1972, more than one-third of the entire US force of B-52 Stratofortress bombers was committed against North Vietnam. The 'big ugly fella', or BUF, delivered huge tonnages of bombs against targets around Hanoi, a task which was made possible by air refuelling from KC-135s. *USAF*

Far left:
Tanker refuelling zones during the Vietnam War.

Maj Alvin L. Lewis introduced earlier in this narrative. Most remarkable of all, however, was the first and perhaps only three-deep refuelling ever made under combat conditions, on 31 May 1967. On that date a KC-135A crew of the 902nd Air Refueling Squadron headed by Maj John H. Casteel was routinely refuelling two F-104 Starfighters over the Gulf of Tonkin when told to contact a Navy ship about a possible emergency. Casteel was vectored towards 'Holly Green Blue' and 'Holly Green White', a pair of US Navy A-3 Skywarriors, themselves tankers from the carrier *Hancock*. The two F-104s escorted the tanker to the scene, receiving refuellings en route.

Upon arrival they discovered that one Skywarrior had only three minutes of fuel left although it had 4,000lb (1,812kg) which it could transfer but not use itself. Casteel refuelled this aircraft sufficiently to keep it going and then hooked up with the second A-3. while this was going on, a TACAN rendezvous was made for two Navy F-8 Crusader fighters from the carrier *Bon Homme Richard*. One of the Crusaders had so little fuel left that he could not wait for the KC-135, but hooked up directly with the A-3 which was still in the process of taking on fuel from the KC-135. While this was happening, the first A-3 shared a portion of his meagre supply with the second F-8 and,

while still connected to the F-8, hooked on to the KC-135.

This confusing but effective method of aerial replenishment became even more confusing when two Navy F-4B Phantoms from the carrier *Constellation* reached the scene with too little fuel to return safely to their ship. Maj Casteel's KC-135 refuelled these, and then refuelled the escorting F-104s once again. Now low on fuel himself, Maj Casteel elected to land at Da Nang Air Base in South Vietnam, which he did safely with 10,000lb (4,535kg) of fuel remaining. During Casteel's incredible mid-air fuel transfer his single KC-135 tanker had furnished 14 refuellings to eight receiver aircraft for a total of almost 50,000lb (22,651kg) of fuel transferred.

If there was an almost comic-opera aspect to Casteel's remarkable set of refuellings, the war itself was grimly serious and became more so. When North Korea seized the American intelligence ship *Pueblo* in January 1968 it appeared for a time that the US might be fighting two wars in Asia simultaneously. On 3 February 1968 the Joint Chiefs of Staff directed the SAC deployment known as 'Port Bow' in support of an air build-up in Korea, sending 26 B-52s and 10 KC-135s to Kadena and to Andersen AB, Guam.

Another big part of the US reaction to the *Pueblo* seizure was deployment of more jet fighters to the Far East, in an operation called 'Combat Fox'. SAC KC-135s supported 'Combat Fox' deployments, the first forces numbering 20, 16, 12 and nine KC-135s respectively. The jet fighters required air refuelling for their task of keeping watch for North Korean MiGs along the 38th Parallel, KC-135s supporting these flights with an average of five tanker operations per day.

Bombing Halt
In the end the 'Rolling Thunder' campaign against North Vietnam came to an ambiguous conclusion when President Johnson announced a 31 October 1968 bombing halt aimed at paving the way for negotiations. For three long years tanker and combat crews had a respite in operations 'up North' until, seeing no progress in peace talks, President Nixon ordered strikes once more against the region around Hanoi. All the while, combat

operations in the south continued to require KC-135A support.

The fight against North Vietnam, and the war itself, ended with the Eleven Day War of 18-29 December 1972 when fully one-third of the US B-52 Stratofortress force was committed to daily missions in the Hanoi region. This was the final struggle. The conflict ended in a negotiated agreement on 27 January 1973. Even then, however, reconnaissance operations continued. KC-135A Stratotankers were employed in various support roles all the way up to the evacuation of Saigon on 30 April 1975.

Although no KC-135A was lost as a result of enemy action, SAC considers four aircraft to be losses in the South-East Asia conflict. On 24 September 1968, KC-135A 55-3133, the 16th Stratotanker built, made an emergency landing at the tiny Wake Island atoll in the Western Pacific. Although the flight crew survived, 11 passengers were killed, all of them members of the 509th Bomb Wing. The wreckage of 55-3133 was a familiar sight to aircrews passing through Wake for

Above:

Toward the end of the South-East Asia conflict, portable shoulder-mounted SAM missiles were in the hands of communist guerrillas. KC-135A Stratotanker crews became accustomed to a sudden, very sharp climb-out after taking off. *USAF*

months afterward, until it was finally disposed of.

The second South-East Asia war loss was KC-135A 55-3138, which crashed on take-off at U-Tapao AB, Thailand, on 1 October 1968. Maj Dean L. Beach and the three other members of the 320th Bomb Wing crew were all killed. On 22 October 1968, aircraft 61-0301 crashed landing on Taiwan, killing six. The final loss was aircraft 56-3629, which also went down at Taiwan, on 19 December 1969, with the loss of four lives.

Not included in the wartime casualty figures is one RC-135 which was lost in the Western Pacific during the Vietnam war but was not on a mission related to the conflict at the time.

9 Tanker

The KC-135 Stratotanker has come a long way. With the 20th century not far from its end, the aircraft has lasted far longer and done much more than anyone ever anticipated, and will still be operating when the year 2000 arrives. Of the 732 tankers built for the US Air Force, no fewer than 648 remain in service today in the air-to-air refuelling role, this figure consisting of 461 KC-135A, five KC-135A relay, four KC-135D, 104 KC-135E, 54 KC-135Q and 20 KC-135R airframes. These of course have now been joined by a small number of Douglas KC-10A Extender aircraft, developed from the civil DC-10 with knowledge based on Stratotanker experience. The American strategic tanker force remains unique in the world, at once both a wonder and an achievement, with no parallel elsewhere. The potential of the tanker force may be exaggerated at times — in a full-scale war, only a small proportion of the warplanes involved would have access to tankers — but it is also too easy, too tempting, to take this force for granted. The capacity to refuel combat aircraft in vast numbers on actual wartime missions is a major national asset, and one of which the United States should be proud.

A brief overview of the Stratotanker force follows, to list its components as of the last date for which details are available.

● **KC-135A** remains the designation for the principal and most important variant of the Stratotanker, in most respects unchanged from the time of its first flight three decades ago.

Serial No	Engine	Used by
461 aircraft (see Appendix 2)	J57-P-59	SAC/ANG/AFRes/various bases
59-1481	J57-P-43	NASA/Houston, Texas

Another aircraft which should properly belong in the chapter on test ships is 59-1481, a KC-135A assigned to NASA to train astronauts in zero-G flying. This aircraft does not have an air refuelling boom installed.

Below:
This Boeing publicity view from the early 1960s shows plain Jane KC-135A Stratotanker 63-8011 in flight over Washington State. Spartan SAC markings were particularly typical of the 1960s and 1970s. *Boeing*

The KC-135A fleet is mostly a collection of 'plain Jane' aircraft in unremarkable markings, often the butt of barrack humour for the smoke clouds kicked up by their J57 engines. The mission of the KC-135A fleet is described officially simply as worldwide refuelling support to bomber, fighter, strategic airlift, reconnaissance and command (SAC) aircraft.

'Combat Lightning'

Included in the KC-135A fleet are veterans of the South-East Asia programme known as 'Combat Lightning'. In June 1966 a requirement was levied upon SAC for airborne radio relay platforms to support the command and control system in South-East Asia. It was at first proposed that this 'Combat Lightning' mission should be carried out by two EC-135L aircraft of the SAC Post Attack Command & Control System (PACCS) fleet, but instead it was decided to employ two standard KC-135A tankers equipped with AN/ARC89 radio gear. The first two, one from Travis AFB, California, and one from Blytheville AFB, Arkansas, were modified by the end of the summer, tested in September and arrived at Kadena AB, Okinawa, on 14 September 1966. Beginning 5 October 1966, the 'Combat Lightning' airframes provided interim radio relay coverage from U-Tapao AB, Thailand. These aircraft flew over the Gulf of Tonkin to relay radio messages to strike and rescue aircraft and to assure that they

were received. This was all done automatically and required no operator or other crew.

To bolster the 'Combat Lightning' fleet, SAC relented and provided two EC-135Ls in May 1967. In addition to carrying regular radio relay equipment, these aircraft were outfitted with secure voice communications gear. With the fleet at four airframes, 24-hour radio relay coverage was provided.

The 'Combat Lightning' fleet eventually numbered five KC-135A aircraft, with the two EC-135Ls returning to the US to resume their command post function. The radio relay force made several moves in the course of the war, operating for a time from Taiwan and Kadena and eventually returning to U-Tapao. The radio relay aircraft performed a number of unusual missions. On 24 October 1972 a fire ravaged the aircraft carrier USS *Midway* (CVA-41) in the Tonkin Gulf. A 'Combat Lightning' aircraft relayed information essential to the evacuation of the seriously wounded on this occasion and the crew was commended for its efforts. On 26 December 1972, during the massive B-52 strikes which brought the conflict to an end, a 'Combat Lightning' aircraft relayed information which proved essential to the destruction of a North Vietnamese MiG-21 stalking the bomber force.

● **KC-135A Relay** is the term given by the US Air Force to the five surviving 'Combat Lightning' aircraft which remain in service. Although included in the overall total of 461 KC-135A airframes in service, they are listed separately. The aircraft carried distinctive radio antennas along the full length of the upper fuselage during their service in the radio relay role, and some can still be identified this way.

Below:
A certain number of SAC tankers remain on strip alert at all times. This view from the 1960s depicts KC-135A 63-7983 of the 301st Air Refueling Wing at Lockbourne AFB, Ohio (now Rickenbacker AFB). *Via M. J. Kasiuba*

Above:
KC-135A Stratotankers powered by the original J57 engines still make up the bulk of the tanker fleet, although all have been through a Boeing modernisation programme. KC-135A 59-1463 sets down at RAF Fairford, England, in 1985. *John Dunnell*

Below:
Almost invisible to the eye are tiny antennae running along the upper fuselage of KC-135A relay aircraft 61-0280. These mark the Stratotanker as a former 'Combat Lightning' relay craft from the South-East Asia conflict. Now a tanker, the KC-135A relay ship is depicted at Mildenhall in April 1985. *Paul Bennett*

Serial No	Engine	Used by
61-268	J57-P-59	384th AREFW/McConnell AFB, Kansas
61-270	J57-P-59	319th BMW/Grand Forks AFB, North Dakota
61-271	J57-P-59	5th BMW/Minot AFB, North Dakota
61-280	J57-P-59	340th AREFG/Altus AFB, Oklahoma
61-303	J57-P-59	97th BMW/Blytheville AFB, Arkansas

Air Force records indicate that these aircraft are still configured for airborne radio relay missions. At present the majority of the avionics equipment has been removed leaving only mounts, wiring and antenna installed. They are used in the normal KC-135A mission with a reduction in total payload due to the higher operating weight of the remaining installed equipment.

● **KC-135D** is the designation assigned to the four tankers which were originally delivered to the Air Force as RC-135As for photo-mapping and geodetic survey work. They are now employed routinely in the standard tanker mission and

warrant their own designation because of minor differences from other tankers.

Serial No	Engine	Used by
63-8058	J57-P-59	305th AREFW/Grissom AFB, Indiana
63-8059	J57-P-59	305th AREFW/Grissom AFB, Indiana
63-8060	J57-P-59	305th AREFW/Grissom AFB, Indiana
63-8061	J57-P-59	305th AREFW/Grissom AFB, Indiana

These aircraft have minor variations in some systems such as anti-skid, communications and air conditioning. Otherwise they are identical to the bulk of the tanker force.

● **KC-135E** is the Air Force designation for aircraft converted from KC-135A by replacement of the J57-P-59 turbojet with the TF33-P-102 turbofan. The Air Force's own table lists them in the following manner:

Serial No	Engine	Used by
104 aircraft (see Appendix 3)	TF33-P-102	SAC/ANG/various bases

38061
U.S. AIR FORCE

63611
OHIO AIR GUARD
U.S. AIR FORCE

ARKANSAS
53141
U.S. AIR FORCE

Assigned to the 305th Air Refueling Wing at Grissom AFB, Indiana, 63-8061 is a KC-135D tanker which was built originally as an RC-135A for photo-mapping and geodetic survey work. In its present-day tanker role it is seen on 5 June 1983. *Paul Bennett*

The KC-135E was retrofitted with TF33 turbofan engines and a Boeing 707 horizontal stabiliser, the turbofans giving the aircraft longer range, greater fuel efficiency and cleaner exhausts. A distinctive feature of the KC-135E is the extra fairing on the inboard engine pylon just above the air intake, as shown on this 145th Air Refueling Squadron, Ohio ANG example seen at RAF Fairford in 1985. *John Dunnell*

Re-engined, turbofan-powered KC-135E Stratotanker 55-3141 of the 189th Air Refueling Group, Arkansas ANG, at its Arkansas lair in 1985. The tandem bogie main landing gear of the Stratotanker is one feature readily visible here. *Arkansas ANG*

This re-engined tanker was intended for Air National Guard use, and all KC-135Es except 59-1514 and 57-2589, which are assigned to SAC, belong to ANG units. The first KC-135E was delivered on 26 January 1982 followed by two months of flight testing at Edwards AFB, California. The modification to KC-135E standard actually involved more than merely re-engining and included additional design, fabrication, refurbishment and cartridge start capability, Boeing 707 horizontal stabilisers, thrust reverser, series yaw damper, improved electrical system and other minor configuration changes related to the new engine. KC-135E 59-1514 is the only machine in this series equipped to receive air-to-air refuelling.

The Air Guardsmen who operate the KC-135E have become most enthusiastic about the aircraft. Performance is markedly improved over the original tanker design and the aircraft is easier to fly and maintain. The civilian warriors who make up the Guard force were once viewed with derision as 'weekend warriors', but in recent years their ranks have become thoroughly professional, in part for the peculiar reason that good men are leaving the Air Force in order to have greater opportunities for military flying! A 1984 study showed that Reservists and Air Guardsmen can actually log more flying hours, often in newer aircraft types, than their active-duty counterparts. At the same time, Guardsmen are relieved of some of the less attractive happenings of regular military life — inspections, paperwork and desk duties.

● **KC-135Q** is the appellation for the tanker aircraft converted for the specific purpose of refuelling the SR-71 Blackbird reconnaissance plane. So different is the Blackbird, requiring a fuel known as JP7 for its J58 engines, that it requires its own tanker. Fifty-six aircraft were converted to KC-135Q standard, two of these being lost, 58-0039 on 3 June 1971 and 60-338 on 2 August 1980. The remaining airframes are shown on the Air Force's table as follows:

Serial No	Engine	Used by
54 aircraft (see Appendix 4)	J57-P-59	SAC/various bases

It is understood that 15 of the 56 KC-135Q Stratotankers are, in fact, 'partial Qs' which perform both regular refuelling and SR-71 refuelling. Again, the size and complexity of the KC-135 family is demonstrated: what appears on most lists as one Stratotanker variant is, in fact, two. Most of the tankers used frequently with the SR-71 are dedicated to the 9th Strategic Reconnaissance Wing at Beale AFB, California, which operates the SR-71 fleet around the world. The usual flying boom system is used but, of course, the fuel is chemically different from that employed by other aircraft and, indeed, by the KC-135Q itself.

● **KC-135R**, a designation used previously to connote a reconnaissance variant, is employed today to refer to the tanker which has been re-engined with F108-CF-100 (CFM-56) engines, the 'fat' powerplants which markedly change the external appearance of the Stratotanker. On 1 July 1985, 20 such airframes were in service, a number which has increased since then, and were listed in the following manner:

Serial No	Engine	Used by
57-1440	F108-CF-100	384th AREFW/McConnell AFB, Kansas
57-1483	F108-CF-100	384th AREFW/McConnell AFB, Kansas
59-1466	F108-CF-100	384th AREFW/McConnell AFB, Kansas
59-1482	F108-CF-100	384th AREFW/McConnell AFB, Kansas
61-293	F108-CF-100	384th AREFW/McConnell AFB, Kansas
61-304	F108-CF-100	384th AREFW/McConnell AFB, Kansas
61-306/313	F108-CF-100	384th AREFW/McConnell AFB, Kansas
61-315	F108-CF-100	384th AREFW/McConnell AFB, Kansas
61-317/318	F108-CF-100	384th AREFW/McConnell AFB, Kansas
61-324	F108-CF-100	384th AREFW/McConnell AFB, Kansas
63-7997	F108-CF-100	384th AREFW/McConnell AFB, Kansas
63-7999	F108-CF-100	384th AREFW/McConnell AFB, Kansas

The first machine in the KC-135R series was originally delivered as a KC-135A and modified in 1965 to an EC-135A. It was modified back to a KC-135A in early 1975 and then modified as the prototype KC-135R in 1982. First flight of a KC-135R was on 4 August 1982 and US Air Force operations began on 2 July 1984.

This variant received a number of new and modified systems when it was converted to the KC-135R configuration. These include dual auxiliary power unit (APU) quick start system, Turbine Engine Monitoring System (TEMS), Flight Control Augmentation System (FCAS), Air

Left:
**A frontal view of re-engined
KC-135E Stratotanker 55-3141 of
the 189th Air Refueling Group,
Arkansas ANG.** *Arkansas ANG*

Below:
**KC-135Q Stratotanker 58-0129,
one of the variant used to refuel the
SR-71 Blackbird in flight, is seen at
RAF Fairford, England, in 1985.**
John Dunnell

Data Computer (ADC), improved landing gear, Mk III anti-skid five-rotor disc brakes, and the F108-CF-100 (CFM 56) engines which develop 24,000lb (11,000kg) of thrust. The KC-135R is significantly quieter than other tankers and far more fuel-efficient.

As noted in the table, the first deliveries were made to the 384th Air Refueling Wing at McConnell AFB, Kansas, just across the runway from the Boeing Military Airplane Co plant where the conversions were made. Since the table was prepared, deliveries began to the 28th Bomb Wing at Ellsworth AFB, South Dakota, on 5 September 1985 when aircraft 59-1453 was delivered from Boeing. The Air Force plans eventually to acquire 393 KC-135R conversions with funds to be allocated through fiscal year 1989.

European aircraft spotters saw the 'fat-engined' KC-135R in June 1986 when the first two examples arrived at RAF Mildenhall, England, on temporary duty with the 306th Strategic Wing. The first two machines in the United Kingdom were 59-1466 and 63-7999, both from McConnell. During their stay at Mildenhall they flew a variety of refuelling and evaluation missions, and local residents were said to be pleased by the quiet, smokeless engines.

Thus ends a roll call of the many variants of the KC-135 Stratotanker, one of the genuinely remarkable aircraft of our time. Now past the ripe age of 30, the KC-135 is only beginning a long and illustrious career, not merely in the air-refuelling role for which it was designed but in a range of other duties and missions. These pages tell the beginning of the KC-135 story but its final chapter lies at least in the next century. Until then the KC-135 will continue to be one of the most visible and best known aircraft types at the world's airfields — an important aircraft, and one deserving of considerable appreciation.

Above:
Aircraft 59-1466 was the first KC-135R to appear outside the US when it showed up at RAF Mildenhall in August 1986. The tanker belongs to the 384th Bomb Wing at McConnell AFB, Kansas. *Paul Bennett*

Below:
The fat CFM56 engines of the KC-135R, as well as the aft-fuselage plexiglass blisters associated with this model, are evident in this view from the rear. Aircraft 61-0293 is thought to be the very first KC-135R delivered to the 384th Bomb Wing at McConnell AFB, Kansas. *USAF*

Appendices

1. KC-135 Stratotankers Manufactured

Model	Amount	From	To	Remarks
KC-135A	29	55-3118	55-3146	Three completed as C-135A; conversions to EC-135A,
	68	56-3591	56-3658	JC-135A, JKC-135A, NC-135A, NKC-135A, RC-135D,
	97	57-1418	57-1514	EC-135G; four converted to VC-135A; three converted
	21	57-2589	57-2609	to EC-135J; three converted to EC-135K; five converted
	130	58-001	58-130	to EC-135L; five converted to EC-135P; 56 converted to
	81	59-1443	59-1523	KC-135Q; four converted to KC-135R; one converted to
	(27)	(58-131)	(58-157)*	KC-135RE; one converted to RC-135T.
	56	60-313	60-368	
	(40)	(60-379)	(60-408)*	
	65	61-261	61-325	
	84	62-3497	62-3580	
	70	63-7976	63-8045	
	18	63-8871	63-8888	
	8	64-14833	64-14840	
Subtotal	727			
C-135A	10	60-369	60-378	Conversions to EC-135N; one converted to VC-135A;
	5	61-326	61-330	one converted to EC-135J; eight converted to EC-135N
				and later to C-135N.
Subtotal	15			
C-135B	2	61-331	61-332	Conversions to WC-135B, VC-135B; one converted to
	13	61-2662	61-2674	RC-135E.
	15	62-4125	62-4139	
Subtotal	30			
KC-135B	5	62-3581	62-3585	17 converted to EC-135C.
	12	63-8046	63-8057	
Subtotal	17			
RC-135A	4	63-8058	63-8061	All converted KC-135D.
	(5)	(63-8062)	(63-8066)*	
Subtotal	4			
C-135F	6	63-8470	63-8475	France.
	6	63-12735	63-12740	
Subtotal	12			
RC-135B	1	63-9792		Conversions to RC-135U, RC-135V; four converted to
	9	64-14841	64-14849	RC-135C.
Subtotal	10			*Contract cancelled.

Model	Amount	From	To	Remarks
EC-135C	5	64-14828	64-14832	
Subtotal	5			
Total	**820**			

2. Boeing 707 Derivatives

Model	Amount	From	To	Remarks
VC-137A	2	58-6970	58-6971	Converted to VC-137B.
Subtotal	2			
VC-137C	1	62-6000		Redesignated C-137C.
	1	72-7000		
Subtotal	2			
C-137C	2	85-6973	85-6974	
Subtotal	2			
EC-137D	2	74-1407	74-1408	Redesignated E-3A.
Subtotal	2			
C-18A	8	81-0891	81-0898	Conversions to EC-18B.
Subtotal	8			
E-3A	2	73-1674	73-1675	Conversions to E-3B.
	6	75-0556	75-0561	
	4	76-1604	76-1607	
	6	77-0351	77-0356	
	3	78-0576	78-0578	
	3	79-0001	79-0003	
	18	79-0442	79-0459	NATO.
	(10)	(25)	(34)	
	5	82-0066	82-0070	Saudi Arabia.
Subtotal	57			
KE-3A	6	82-0071	82-0076	Saudi Arabia.
	2	83-0510	83-0518	
Subtotal	8			
E-6A	(8)	(1)	(8)	
Subtotal	8			
Total	**89**			

3. KC-135 and Boeing 707 Military Variants

C-135A Transport, J57 engines, 15 built plus three converted, two in service in 1985.

C-135B Transport, TF33 engines, 30 built, five in service in 1985.

C-135C Transport conversion of ex-C-135B, ex-WC-135B, TF33 engines, three in service in 1985.

C-135E Test aircraft, TF33 engines, three in service in 1985, one to be converted to NC-135E.

C-135F Transport/tanker for France, J57 engines, 12 built, one lost, 11 converted to C-135FR.

C-135FR Transport/tanker for France, refitted with CFM56 engines, 11 converted.

C-135N ARIA aircraft. *See* EC-135N.

C-137A Redesignation of VC-137A.

C-137B Redesignation of VC-137B.

C-137C Redesignation of VC-137C.

C-18A Boeing 707, eight purchased, at least four converted to EC-18B.

EC-135A SAC 'Looking Glass' command post, J57 engines, five in service in 1985.

EC-135B Convertion of ex-C-135B as ex-ARIA, TF33 engines, to be converted to RC-135X.

EC-135C SAC command post, TF33 engines, 13 in service in 1985.

EC-135E ARIA conversion from EC-135N, TF33 engines, four in service in 1985.

EC-135G SAC ICBM launch and radio link command post, J57 engines, four in service in 1985.

EC-135H SAC command post, TF33 engines, five in service in 1985.

EC-135J PACAF command post, four in service in 1985.

EC-135K TAC command post, TF33 engines, three converted, two in service in 1985.

EC-135L Special SAC relay platform, TF33 engines, five in service in 1985.

EC-135N ARIA aircraft, ex-C-135A, later C-135N, later C-135E.

EC-135P Communications/command post, three in service in 1985.

EC-135Y US Army command post, J57 engines, one converted.

EC-137D Two converted from Boeing 707-320B as prototype for E-3A.

E-3A Boeing 707 derivative AWACS aircraft, 34 to USAF, 18 to NATO, five to Saudi Arabia (with KE-3A).

E-3B Upgrade of E-3A.

E-3C Upgrade of E-3A.

E-6A Projected US Navy TACAMO command post converted from Boeing 707 with F108 (CFM56) engines.

EC-18B Conversion of C-18A to ARIA configuration.

KC-135A Standard tanker, J57 engines, 461 in service in 1985.

KC-135B Tanker, TF33 engines.

KC-135D Tanker conversion of ex-RC-135A, four in service in 1985.

KC-135E Tanker conversion of KC-135A, TF33 engines, 104 in service in 1985.

KC-135R First use of this designation was for recce/EW aircraft, two converted.

KC-135R Tanker conversion of KC-135A, F108 engines.

Below:
KC-135A Stratotanker 63-8025 of the 305th Bomb Wing was photographed at RAF Mildenhall, England, in mid-1986. *Paul Bennett*

KE-3A Tanker/AWACS Boeing 707 derivative for Saudi Arabia, CFM56 engines, eight to be delivered (with five E-3A).

NC-135A Test aircraft.

NC-135E Forthcoming conversion of one C-135E to laser testbed.

NKC-135A Test fleet for ECM/ECCM, laser, vulnerability, icing, comsat and other research, 11 in service in 1985.

RC-135A Mapping and survey reconnaissance aircraft, four built, all converted to KC-135D.

RC-135B Reconnaissance derivative, TF33 engines, SLAR cheeks, other sensors, 10 built.

RC-135C Recce, TF33 engines, SLAR cheeks, 10 converted.

RC-135D Recce, J57 engines, different SLAR, thimble nose, four converted.

RC-135E Recce, TF33 engines, glass fibre forward fuselage and inboard wing pods, one converted.

RC-135M Recce, numerous electronic installations, TF33 engines, six converted, one converted to RC-135W.

RC-135R Redesignation of KC-135R recce aircraft.

RC-135S Recce, similar to M with additional installations, TF33 engines, three converted, two in service in 1985.

RC-135T Trainer for recce crews, one converted.

RC-135U Recce, TF33 engines, special sensors and aerials, SLAR cheeks, extended tailcone, three converted, two in service in 1985.

RC-135V Recce, TF33 engines, rebuild of seven Cs and one U with nose thimble, wire aerials, ventral blades, eight in service in 1985.

RC-135W Recce, TF33 engines, rebuilt from M with SLAR cheeks, inverted T-shaped antenna under fuselage, six converted.

RC-135X Forthcoming recce variant, TF33 engines.

RC-135S Conversion of Ex-C-135B, ex-EC-135B, one in service in 1985.

VC-135B VIP transport, TF33 engines.

VC-137A Boeing 707-153, JT3C engines, three built, converted to VC-137B.

VC-137B Conversion from VC-137A with JT3D fan engines.

VC-137C Transport, Boeing 707-353B, two delivered, two on order.

WC-135B Standard MAC weather recce platform.

4. KC-135A Aircraft in Service as of 1 July 1985

Total Aircraft — 461

55-3130	57-1432	58-001	58-108/58-110
55-3136	57-1435/57-1437	58-004/58-005	58-113/58-114
55-3137	57-1439	58-009/58-010*	58-116
55-3139	57-1441	58-013/58-016	58-118/58-123
55-3142	57-1447	58-018*	58-124*
55-3145	57-1451	58-020/58-021	58-126*
56-3591/56-3592	57-1453/57-1454	58-023	58-128
56-3594/56-3595	57-1456	58-025	58-130
56-3600/56-3601	57-1459	58-027/58-030	59-1443/59-1447
56-3603	57-1461/57-1462	58-033/58-038	59-1449
56-3608	57-1467	58-041	59-1451/59-1455
56-3610	57-1469/57-1474	58-044	59-1458/59-1459
56-3614/56-3617	57-1476/57-1477	58-051/58-053	59-1461
56-3619/56-3621	57-1479	58-056	59-1463
56-3623/56-3625	57-1486/57-1488	58-058/58-059	59-1469
56-3627	57-1490	58-063/58-064	59-1472
56-3632/56-3637	57-1492/57-1493	58-066	59-1475/59-1478
56-3639	57-1497	58-070	59-1481 (no boom)
56-3642	57-1499	58-073	59-1483
56-3644/56-3647	57-1502	58-075/58-076	59-1486
56-3649	57-1504	58-079	59-1488
56-3651/56-3653	57-1508	58-081/58-083	59-1493/59-1494
56-3656	57-1511/57-1512	58-085	59-1495/59-1496
57-1418/57-1420	57-1514	58-090/58-093	59-1498
57-1422/57-1423	57-2590/57-2593	58-097/58-098	59-1500/59-1503
57-1427	57-2596/57-2603	58-100	59-1506/59-1508
57-1430	57-2605	58-102	59-1511
	57-2609	58-104/58-106	59-1515/59-1517

59-1521/59-1522
60-313/60-329
60-330/60-334
60-341
60-347/60-351
60-353
60-355
60-356*/60-357*
60-358/60-361
60-362*
60-363/60-367
61-264

61-266/61-268
61-270/61-272
61-275/61-277
61-280/61-281
61-284
61-288
61-290
61-292
61-294/61-295
61-298/61-300
61-302/61-303
61-305

61-314
61-319/61-323
61-325
61-320/61-321
61-323/61-325
62-3497/62-3521
62-3523/62-3534
62-3537/62-3569
62-3571/62-3578
62-3580
63-7976/63-7988
63-7990/63-7993

63-7995/63-7996
63-7998/63-8000
63-8002/63-8041
63-8043/63-8045
63-8871/63-8881
63-8883/63-8888
64-14828/64-14840

*Air Refuelling Receiver
System installed.

Below:
**KC-135A 56-3611, with the distinctive markings of the
Ohio ANG (also found on the ruddevator of the refuelling
boom), settles down at RAF Fairford, England, in 1985.**
John Dunnell

5. KC-135E Aircraft in Service as of 1 July 1985

Total Aircraft — 104

55-3141	57-1428/57-1429	57-1495/57-1496	58-0087
55-3143	57-1431	57-1501	58-0096
55-3146	57-1433	57-1503	58-0107
55-3593	57-1434	57-1505/57-1507	58-0111
56-3604	57-1438	57-1509/57-1510	58-0115
56-3606/56-3607	57-1443	57-2589	59-1448
56-3609	57-1445	57-2594/57-2595	59-1450
56-3611	57-1448	57-2604	59-1456/59-1457
56-3612	57-1450	57-2606/57-2608	59-1473
56-3622	57-1452	58-0003	59-1479
56-3626	57-1455	58-0006	59-1484/59-1485
56-3630/56-3631	57-1458	58-0008	59-1487
56-3638	57-1460	58-0012	59-1489
56-3640/56-3641	57-1463/57-1465	58-0017	59-1494
56-3643	57-1468	58-0024	59-1497
56-3648	57-1475	58-0032	59-1499
56-3650	57-1478	58-0040	59-1505
56-3654	57-1480/57-1481	58-0043	59-1509
56-3658	57-1482	58-0057	59-1514
57-1421	57-1484/57-1485	58-0067/58-0068	59-1519
57-1425/57-1426	57-1491	58-0078	
	57-1494	58-0080	

6. KC-135Q Aircraft in Service as of 1 July 1985

Total Aircraft — 54

58-042	58-077	58-129	59-1510
58-045/58-047	58-084	59-1460	59-1512/59-1513
58-049/58-050	58-086	59-1462	59-1520
58-054/58-055	58-088/58-089	59-1464	59-1523
58-060/58-062	58-094/58-095	59-1467/59-1468	60-335/60-337
58-065	58-099	59-1470/59-1471	60-339
58-069	58-103	59-1474	60-342/60-346
58-071/58-072	58-112	59-1480	
58-074	58-117	59-1490	
	58-125	59-1504	

7. US Air Force KC-135 Units

US Air Force, Air Force Reserve and Air National Guard units operating the KC-135 as of 31 October 1986

Unit	Location
Air Force Reserve (AFRes)	
314 ARS/904 ARG	Mather AFB, California
72 ARS/931 ARG	Grissom AFB, Indiana
336 ARS/452 ARW	March AFB, California
Air National Guard (ANG)	
191 ARS/157 ARG	Salt Lake City, Utah
197 ARS/161 ARF	Phoenix Airport, Arizona
154 ARS/189 ARG	Little Rock AFB, Arkansas

Unit	Location
151 ARS/134 ARG	Knoxville Airport, Tennessee
159 ARS/170 ARG	McGuire AFB, New Jersey
147 ARS/171 ARW	Pittsburg-Coreapolis, Pennsylvania
145 ARS/180 ARG	Rickenbacker AFB, Ohio
133 ARS/157 ARG	Pease AFB, New Hampshire
132 ARS/101 ARW	Bangor, Maine
126 ARS/129 ARG	Mitchell Field, Wisconsin
117 ARS/190 ARG	Forbes ANGB, Kansas
116 ARS/141 ARW	Fairchild AFB, Washington
108 ARS/126 ARW	Chicago, Illinois

Unit	Location	Unit	Location
Strategic Air Command — Fifteenth Air Force		407 ARS/42 BMW	Loring AFB, Maine
28 ARS/28 BMW	Ellsworth AFB, South Dakota	42 ARS/42 BMW	Loring AFB, Maine
		305 ARS/305 ARW	Grissom AFB, Indiana
906 ARS/5 BMW	Minot AFB, North Dakota	70 ARS/305 ARW	Grissom AFB, Indiana
904 ARS/320 BMW	Mather AFB, California	97 ARS/96 BMW	Blytheville AFB, Arkansas
92 ARS/92 BMW	Fairchild AFB, Washington	911 ARS/68 ARG	Seymour Johnson AFB,
924 ARS/93 BMW	Castle AFB, California		North Carolina
350 ARS/9 SRW	Beale AFB, California	912 ARS/19 ARW	Robins AFB, Georgia
349 ARS/9 SRW	Beale AFB, California	99 ARS/19 ARW	Robins AFB, Georgia
917 ARS/96 BMW	Dyess AFB, Texas	71 ARS/2 BMW	Barksdale AFB, Louisiana
22 ARS/22 ARW	March AFB, California	41 ARS/416 BMW	Griffiths AFB, New York
905 ARS/319 BMW	Grand Forks AFB, North Dakota	307 ARS/410 BMW	K. I. Sawyer AFB, Michigan
		46 ARS/410 BMW	K. I. Sawyer AFB, Michigan
909 ARS/376 SW	Kadena AB, Okinawa	920 ARS/379 BMW	Wurtsmith AFB, Michigan
		384 ARS/384 ARW	McConnell AFB, Kansas
Strategic Air Command — Eighth Air Force		91 ARS/384 ARW	McConnell AFB, Kansas
509 ARS/509 BMW	Pease AFB, New Hampshire	340 ARS/340 ARW	Altus AFB, Oklahoma
280 ARS/380 BMW	Plattsburgh AFB, New York	11 ARS/340 ARW	Altus AFB, Oklahoma
310 ARS/380 BMW	Plattsburgh AFB, New York	7 ARS/7 BMW	Carswell AFB, Texas

Above:
The Pennsylvania ANG at Pittsburgh is the operator of this KC-135E Stratotanker (59-1457), seen touching down during a trip abroad. The SAC band around the fuselage is the most familiar marking on these tankers, which often look like plain Janes compared to other aircraft with colourful insignia. *John Dunnell*

Overleaf:
A present-day 'customer' for the KC-135 Stratotanker is the Fairchild A-10A Warthog attack aircraft. A fighter wing of 108 A-10A aircraft at RAF Woodbridge/Bentwaters, England, would be unable to operate against Warsaw Pact targets from its home base unless air-to-air refuelling was employed. *USAF*